CHURCH RESET

© Copyright 2020 Focus Press, Inc. and Jack Wilkie
International Standard Book Number 978-0-9796356-1-8

Cover design: Nick Long
Interior Design: Michael Whitworth
Cover Image: © Getty

For information or to order copies of
Church Reset: God's Design for so Much More
contact the publisher:

FOCUS PRESS
625 Bakers Bridge Avenue, Suite 105
Franklin, Tennessee 37067
focuspress.org

Library of Congress cataloging-in-publication
Jack Wilkie (1989-)
Includes Biblical references
ISBN 978-0-9796356-1-8
1. Religion. 2. Christian Family. 3. Parenting.

CONTENTS

DEDICATION

To Allison, my wonderful wife and co-laborer for the Gospel. This book would not have happened without your steadfast encouragement.

ACKNOWLEDGEMENTS

To Mom, Dad, Rachel, Anna, and Joe for reading chapters, giving feedback, and listening to me talk for countless hours as I fleshed out my thoughts.

To Brad Harrub for supporting the project from day one and helping me get it published.

To Michael Whitworth for reading chapters, giving feedback, and helping navigate the book's production.

To Nick Long for designing a cover that captures the book's idea so well.

To Tonja McRady and her wonderful proofreading skills for catching my errors and making me look good.

To Edwin Jones and everyone else who read chapters and gave feedback. Your insights were invaluable.

To all who have taken time to share their experiences stepping beyond "churchianity," your stories have given me great hope and excitement for the future.

To all who joined in on discussions on the Church Reset Facebook page for motivating me to keep going and for contributing valuable perspectives.

INTRODUCTION

MOST OF US DON'T remember learning how to speak. At some point, we started with one word and have continued learning words and how to use them ever since. We learned from an early age that if we want to understand what's happening around us and help others understand us, we need to communicate accurately through our choice of words. But what if we were to learn a word incorrectly? In that case, we would continue to think of and use the word incorrectly until someone corrected us or until we came across an example of it being used properly. For example, in her early speaking days my toddler often excitedly referred to orange as "apppoes!" After a few weeks of corrections— "No, this is an orange and that is an apple"—she came to understand that apples are green and red and taste a certain way, while oranges are, well, orange and taste much differently. If we hadn't said anything she'd still be calling them by the wrong names. Is it possible this is what happened to us with the word "church"? Did our understanding of what church means come from the Bible, or from the picture we were given as children or as new converts?

When we talk about the church, are we referring to it the same way God intended, or are we calling oranges apples?

Let me illustrate it another way, this time with the universal language of food. My favorite food in the world is Nashville hot chicken. A cousin introduced me to its spicy goodness a few years ago and I've been hooked ever since. The problem is, I don't live in Nashville. I don't live within 500 miles of Nashville. You would think that with its ever-increasing popularity I'd be able to find a suitable replica in the Dallas area, but every attempt I've found totally missed the mark.

In mentioning it to friends I've often been asked what exactly Nashville hot chicken is. I can tell them that it's a very specific type of spicing that heavily features cayenne pepper. Other than that, though, I couldn't really tell you what it is. What I can tell you is what it's not. With every one I've tried around here I could instantly point out why they didn't do it right.

When looking at the Bible's picture of the church I've often had the same feeling. I couldn't put my finger on what exactly church should look like, but I've always had a nagging feeling that what I've known and what I've been a part of is not what it's supposed to look like. Of course, it's not terribly important that I ever figure out how to properly explain and describe Nashville hot chicken. Being able to come up with a Biblical picture of the church, on the other hand, is something that matters greatly. So, a few years ago I set out to read and listen to everything I could find about the church. I studied the Bible's picture of the church deeply. I spoke with others who have been a part of different church structures.

So, *Church Reset* is the result of years of studying, reading, and conversing on the topic of the church because I and the others I was speaking to and learning from couldn't shake the feeling that God had something different in mind for His people. Rather than just pointing out what I thought it shouldn't be, I hoped to find out and start working toward a picture of what it could be.

Before I share the conclusions of my study, a few disclaimers seem necessary.

WHAT THIS BOOK IS NOT:

This book is not written for church leaders only.

This book is for any Christian. There will be parts that speak more directly toward leadership, but overall it's my prayer that any Christian who picks up this book can gain from what they read and use the practical suggestions offered at the end. It's for the Christian who feels like God had something more in mind for the church than what we know today.

This book is not meant to bash the church.

I want to say right up front that I love the church and could not feel more blessed to be a part of it. I have no intention of bashing Christ's bride with the critiques offered in this book. The very idea that there must be something more to church than what we commonly see today is one that many will view as negative and critical, though. The point of this type of discussion is not to be negative or critical. In fact, it's quite the opposite.

The distinction comes down to how we're using the word church. If by the word we mean God's perfectly planned institution, then there's no room for change or criticism because He does all things well. If, on the other hand, we're discussing church from the angle of what we as humans have done with it, then there is always room for improvement. With that second use in mind, if my hypothesis is true and there is more to be found in church than what we currently see, then by necessity something would have to change. In a sense, we would be attempting to move away from the second in pursuit of the first.

The point, then, is to believe God has even greater blessings to give us if we abandon the business-like practices that have crept into the church and turn instead toward more mission-driven, family-driven lives. It's the belief that the kind of love and unity we see early on in Acts is attainable today. It's the belief that our personal walk with God can reach a whole other level when we share our lives with our fellow Christians as God meant for us to do.

To view that as negative would be a mistake. It's nothing short of thrilling to consider what kind of love, service, outreach, and growth can happen when we get back to doing things God's way.

This book is not meant to address every single situation.

Before the charge is brought up, I freely admit that much of what is written in this book could be called painting with a broad brush. Because every situation is different I can only start from a generic picture of the modern American church. Some of the critiques and characterizations offered will not apply to you or your church. Some of the changes suggested from the Scriptures might be things you are already practicing. I can't possibly know every situation, which means I can't possibly address every situation. So, I'm trusting you as the reader to take what applies to your situation and make use of it as you will.

On the other hand, I ask you to keep an open mind. While realizing that not everything written here may apply directly to you, don't go so far as to assume that nothing is of use to you. In raising some of the points you'll see in the book I've received responses along the lines of "Yes, that's what my church already does!" when it's plainly evident that such a claim isn't true. While the broad brush can not reach every intricate detail, it is still aimed at reaching that which is broadly true. So, take it for what it's worth and evaluate each point on its own merit with regard to your situation.

This book is not an attempt to write the next big church growth strategy book.

This is not me writing as the next in a line of megachurch leaders sharing the new thing that will make your church boom. In a sense, it's quite the opposite. I'm part of a small church that's not looking for the next big thing but rather working toward getting back to the simplicity with which the church first began. For that reason, it's my hope that the ideas shared in this book aren't new at all. Rather than being a church growth book, it's intended as an ecclesiology book — a study of the Bible's portrayal of the church.

As part of the churches of Christ, restorationism is in my blood. It's my belief that much good work has been done with regard to restoring New Testament doctrine. However, it's also my belief that we have more to do when it comes to restoring New Testament practice. So, rather than being "Jack Wilkie's 3 Step Method to Growing Your Church," this book is first and foremost the result of a multi-year study on the church. I'm sharing what I've learned by study and experience in hopes that it blesses others.

I certainly believe that doing things in the way God prescribed will lead to growth (both internal and numerical), but that's not the same thing as "Try this method and you'll get lots of people." The important thing is to focus on process and not result. God gives the increase (1 Corinthians 3:6). It's left to us to leave that part to Him and be faithful to His way of doing things. That's the aim of this book.

This book is not meant to be a manual.

Though there is a discussion of practical actions churches as a whole and individual members can and should take toward the end of the book, I'm not writing to give a step by step guide. I am not writing as the person who has all the answers. I'm just hoping to share Biblical princi-pals that in my view have been overlooked and neglected over the years. Whether you agree with them and how you decide to act on them is left to you, the reader.

It's my prayer that this book is a blessing to you. More than anything I hope it helps you love Jesus more by appreciating the beauty of His plan for His bride.

1

SHOULDN'T CHURCH BE...MORE?

> Now, therefore, you are no longer strangers and foreign-
> ers, but fellow citizens with the saints and members of the
> household of God, having been built on the foundation
> of the apostles and prophets, Jesus Christ Himself being
> the chief cornerstone, in whom the whole building, be-
> ing fitted together, grows into a holy temple in the Lord,
> in whom you also are being built together for a dwelling
> place of God in the Spirit.
>
> Ephesians 2:19-22

HAVE YOU EVER had one of those experiences where you go in with high expectations only to be totally let down?

A certain mouse-hosted theme park located in Florida was that way for me. Through my entire childhood I saw TV commercials telling me just how magical a place it was. I heard athletes gleefully exclaiming that they were going there after winning championships. I was well familiar with the park's self-given description as a place of happiness unmatched anywhere in the world. But while I enjoyed the visit when I had the chance to go, on the trip home I couldn't help but think "...That's it?"

Those magic-filled commercials somehow neglected to depict the hours-long lines. They didn't tell you that at the end of those lines would be rides which differ little from the average ride at your local amusement park, except for a few beloved characters thrown in the scenery. And when they tell you about how happy everyone is while there, they conveniently leave out all the overheated, exhausted toddlers pitifully on the verge of meltdown or the occasional family yelling at each other because they can't agree on where to go next. Obviously I didn't really expect it to be *the* happiest place, but with such a lofty description I at least expected it to be happier than most other places I've been. It's not like it was unenjoyable. It's just that after such inflated expectations, I couldn't help but be left with that question—"...That's it?"

I can't tell you how often I've returned home on a Sunday night after 3 sessions of worship and study and thought "...That's it?" Each week I preach a sermon knowing full well that most of it won't be retained and having little to no opportunity to sit down with individuals and discuss the text with them, hear their questions, and learn from their input. Each week we stay conscious of the clock on the wall, sticking to our programmed 6 songs, 2 prayers, Scripture reading, sermon, Lord's Supper, and giving format because some (perhaps many) people wouldn't come if we left it open-ended. Each week I have those exchanges I've come to hate: "How are you?" "Good, how are you?" "Good." —exchanges which give no opportunity for building each other up and bearing each other's burdens. Shouldn't church be more?

It's at this point you might start to think, maybe my expectations are too high. Maybe like with Disney World I'm expecting some kind of unattainable ideal. The difference is, our expectations for the church weren't cooked up by some brilliant, high-dollar marketing firm. They come from God's inspired Word. Consider just a few of the glimpses the Bible gives us of what God intended the church to be.

THE ACTS 2 CHURCH

The first Scripture to come to mind for most will be that tight-knit group who began the church in Acts 1-2. Pre-Pentecost they gathered together and devoted themselves to prayer (Acts 1:14). Afterward, once the Spirit had been received and the 3,000 had been baptized, they all immediately became family. They were devoted to the apostles' teaching, to fellowshipping with one another, to the breaking of bread, and to prayer. Those who were more well off started selling property to take care of those of their group who were in need. They shared meals together and gathered in each other's houses as they praised God together. They were a *family* in every sense.

How many times have you read that section and thought, "Why can't it be that way?" Unfortunately, too often our first response to that question is why it can't be that way. "We're a lot busier now." "It's not realistic." And yes, it's true that not everything they did was sustainable even for them. But if you have that nagging feeling that their example is much closer to what God wants for His people and that their lives were a reflection of what His eternal kingdom will look like when it is fully realized, then those simple, wave-of-the-hand explanations aren't going to satisfy.

Every time I read Acts 2 and compare the way church looked then to the way it looks now, the question keeps tugging at me—shouldn't church be… more? It's like having a homesickness for a place we've never been or a nostalgia for an era we didn't actually experience.

THE PROMISE TO PETER

Though Acts 2 is often dismissed as an unattainable ideal that was unsustainable and should not be expected today, the beginning of Acts isn't the only section in the Bible which hints God intended a bigger, richer experience of church than what we know.

Consider what Jesus promised Peter in Mark 10. Right on the heels of the rich young ruler rejecting Jesus in order to hang on to his wealth, Peter points out that he and his apostle colleagues had left everything to follow Jesus. Jesus didn't just say "Yeah, but you get to go to Heaven when you die." No, the reward for such sacrifice was this:

> Assuredly, I say to you, there is no one who has left house or brothers or sisters or father or mother or wife or children or lands, for My sake and the gospel's, who shall not receive a hundredfold now in this time—houses and brothers and sisters and mothers and children and lands, with persecutions—and in the age to come, eternal life.
>
> Mark 10:29-30

Essentially His message was "the family you receive from following Me will be more than worth it." As one commentary put it,

He who forsakes his own for the sake of Christ will find others, many in number, who will give him the love of brethren and sisters, with even greater affection; so that he will seem not to have lost or forsaken his own, but to have received them again with interest. For spiritual affections are far deeper than natural; and his love is stronger who burns with heavenly love which God has kindled, than he who is influenced by earthly love only, which only nature has planted.

In a society like ours where the family has been downplayed and devalued, we've become very casual with the concept of family. We have our "work family." The people who share in our kids' hobbies are our "baseball family," "theater family," or "band family." Therefore, when speaking of the "church family," it's easy to relegate it to that definition of "people who share a common interest but aren't our *actual* family."

Jesus, on the other hand, expected the church to be a family that exceeded by a hundred fold the families who might forsake his followers. Remember that theirs was a culture in which, unlike ours, family was everything. Being asked to forsake their own blood for Jesus (Matthew 10:34-37) placed a massive price on discipleship and yet it was in that context Jesus promised them a family which would be worth it 100 times over. Often this is explained by pointing out that we'll be spending eternity with our spiritual family whereas the physical family only lasts for this lifetime. While that's true, the point is much bigger than that. As the commentator points out, we should have every expectation that the love which flows from God's Spirit (Galatians 5:22) will be far more powerful than our natural, human love.

What would it look like if that were true? Look once again to Acts 2. They immediately went about the business of loving and caring for each other in the way Jesus intended. Didn't their love for each other look exactly like the fulfillment of what Jesus had promised?

While we've all likely had glimpses and tastes of this kind of family in the church, that kind of life-sharing connection is the exception rather than the rule in modern American churches. It's something we'll only experience if church is more.

A FAMILY LOST

Another example—consider Jesus' plan for church discipline. In Matthew 18 He outlines how to confront sin and the church's last resort is to "let him be to you as a Gentile and a tax collector" (18:17). His first century audience would have heard that as "don't go anywhere near him. Keep him out of your fellowship."

Paul applied this exhortation to the man who was fornicating with his father's wife in 1 Corinthians 5. He commanded the congregation to hand the man over to Satan, to not associate with him, and to purge the evil person from their midst, using language borrowed from the Law when God wanted them to remove corrupting influences from their camp or their land. He used the language of withdrawal yet again in 2 Thessalonians 3 to refer to those who were unruly and refusing to work. Removal of fellowship was a serious tool Jesus wanted His church to use to bring about repentance.

The natural implication, of course, is that the fellowship and love of the church would be so valuable and so sorely missed that it would be hurtful to have it taken from one's life. Where threat of eternal punishment is sometimes too distant to motivate people, showing them the immediate price tag of sin through the loss of family is God's way of showing the sinner just how painful sin is. However, if the threat were simply "You have to go somewhere else on Sunday"—essentially what it amounts to now—the correction would hold little chance of effecting change. When Christ's church is such a small part of its peoples' lives, having it taken away feels like a rather small cost.

However, if the church were something more, if it were truly the family and support system we see in the Scriptures, being cut off from such a situation would be devastating. The distinction between being part of the church and separated from it would be noticeably different, which was clearly God's intention.

In the institutional, business-like model of church, the guilty party can simply move on to the next one, akin to getting kicked out of McDonald's and walking across the street to Wendy's. But if there exists within a congregation something that simply can't be found elsewhere because it is powered by God and shared among people who have sacrificed everything for Christ, one can't just replace that by driving to join a church down the street or in the next town. It only works this way if church is more.

We could continue making this point through the Scriptures by going to the Old Testament prophecies of the kingdom, or Jesus' parables about the pearl and the hidden treasure (Matt. 13:44-46), or Paul's description of the church as Christ's bride (Eph. 5:22-33). I won't belabor the point, though. It doesn't take much study to realize that individualistic, consumeristic, Sunday (and maybe Wednesday) meetings of loosely connected people was not what God intended.

WHAT IF...?

It's hard to describe what I'm speaking about in practical terms though because we see so little of it. In trying to give a description, people often respond "That's how my church is! We're friendly and help each other out if anybody is in need." I don't doubt that some churches are closer than others. However, over the last few years of writing and speaking on this topic I've heard from a few people who are a part of (or have previously been a part of) the kind of church that is just... more.

I've heard their stories about churches who were so tight-knit that they all had a 24-7 open door policy which was regularly exercised, just showing up on each other's doorsteps from time to time and being accepted in for whatever help was needed. I've heard stories of congregations where every member is a valuable contributor, where nobody is a detached customer but rather every person is seen as a Jesus follower who God will strengthen to carry out His purposes. I've heard stories of churches where prayers for the church's work were answered so directly and so regularly that it was undeniable that God's hand was directly involved in the congregation's work. Their stories just about give me chills as I think of the jaw-dropping ways that God came through for them. I've heard stories of congregations who gather on Sunday with essentially no clock on the wall, spending each Lord's Day together like a weekly family reunion rather than as a gathering that has a hard limit on how long they will worship, fellowship, and study. As they share their experiences, you can instantly tell they aren't just talking about a church that is friendlier than other ones they've been a part of, or one that has perfected some evangelistic system. In their explanations there's an implied message of, "No, no, you don't understand. This was different. This was powerful, life-changing, and I've never seen anything like it anywhere else." In hearing from them I can't help but think of Acts 2:43—"Everyone kept feeling a sense of awe" (NASB). How often is awe—Biblical, fearful, praise-inducing awe— something we feel as part of church life?

Our first instinct might be to start hedging by pointing out challenges that might arise. We might concede that a lot of people wouldn't be interested in that much fellowship. We might start making the case as to why these things are impractical. But before we shut it down, doesn't that sound so much more like the kind of church the Bible describes? Doesn't God expect that kind of love and sacrifice for each other and promise us we'll be blessed if we do it?

Consider a few more questions regarding this idea that there is something greater and higher than what we typically see.

- What if we took Paul's metaphor of a body seriously, realizing that we are as interconnected as limbs and torso, that we feel each other's pain, that we can't fully function without each part contributing (1 Corinthians 12, Ephesians 4)?

- What if we took the "one another" commands (love one another, serve one another, give preference to one another) as seriously as the "thou shalt not" commands?

- What if we realized that passively listening to lessons three to four hours per week and "being there every time the doors are open" does not constitute being an active member of the church?

- What if we assumed the very serious task of being responsible for the spiritual wellbeing of the people in our church family (Galatians 6:1-2, Hebrews 3:12-14)?

- What if we embraced God's strength in our weaknesses (2 Corinthians 12:9-10) by regularly confessing sins and sharing our struggles?

- What if we dropped the perfect facade and got to know each other's lives beyond the superficial "How are you doing?" "Good, you?" "Good" conversations?

- What if we were all close enough to each other that we would be able to correct and rebuke each other when needed rather than keeping silent or gossiping to others about problems that arise?

- What if we lived like we're dependent on the constant prayers of our church family and they are dependent on ours? Constant prayers…not just when we're sick or traveling, but in living out Christlikeness every day.

- What if we believed in the power of God to accomplish His own purposes, that Christ's name would be taken to all creation through us?

- What if we lived with the understanding that our homes, our time, and our resources all belong to God for His purposes as we've signed our lives over as living and holy sacrifices (Romans 12:1)?

- What if we took seriously the command to be hospitable (Romans 12:13)?

- What if we tried to attract people with the beauty of Jesus rather than programs, events, and services that make them into customers?

- What if we measured success by how many people we equip and send rather than how many people sit in the pews?

- What if we spent less time talking about the evils of the world and more time reaching out to them in love?

- What if Sunday was less of a set time to come, worship, and be done (and certainly never go over time) and more of a weekly family reunion around our Father's table?

- What if we acted on the belief that "church" is neither a building nor an event but instead *we are* the church?

- What if we were willing to put every non-Biblical tradition (programs, Sunday evening, Wednesday evening, order of worship, etc.) on the table and review it for its value in carrying out the mission and being pleasing to God?

- What if we realized that we are not just a collection of individuals trying to live moral lives so we can go to Heaven? What if we realized the Bible itself wasn't written to individuals but to a peculiar people?

- What if we really did love each other in the same extreme, sacrificial manner that Jesus loves the church (John 13:34-35) and treated each other accordingly?

- What if we grasped that merely getting along while we are in the building together and being friendly to visitors doesn't make for a "loving church" in the way that God intended?

- What if our goal was to be known primarily for this radical love rather than our perfect doctrine, great preaching, lively singing, nice building, or attractive programs? What if we believed

Jesus when He said that this loving unity would be the mark of a Christian (John 13:35) and our apologetic to make the world believe in Him (John 17:20-21)?

- How would church be different if our congregations made an all-out effort to restore the Acts 2:42-47 brand of church fellowship, hospitality, and love?

I firmly believe a church life that is more is attainable. It's not attainable because I have all the answers and if you follow me and my model it'll all work out. That's not the point, and I don't offer this book as a solution from somebody who has all the answers. I don't write as the expert but as the student. I'm simply starting from this premise—one I believe to be Biblical—that God intended so much more for us in His church than the business-like model most commonly seen today.

The answer isn't to come up with an answer—it's to get out of the way and let God lead. By knowing His commands, determining to follow them, and letting Him strengthen us for the task, more starts to come into picture.

DISCUSSION QUESTIONS

1. Have you ever felt that church was meant to be more than what we typically know? In what way(s)?
2. If Paul were to spend a week with your church, what would stand out to him as different?
3. What's one way you can bring more Christ-like love into your church life?

GOING OUT OF BUSINESS

> In the beginning the church was a fellowship of men and women centering on the living Christ. Then the church moved to Greece, where it became a philosophy. Then it moved to Rome, where it became an institution. Next it moved to Europe where it became a culture, and, finally, it moved to America where it became an enterprise.
>
> Unknown Origin[1]

THE CHALLENGE AT the very heart of writing a book on "resetting" the modern church is this: how do I decide to whom I'm writing? Is it for church leaders or for church members? For people who have a vested interest in running the church or for church attendees?

That such a distinction exists is not merely one of a number of areas that must be addressed. No, it's *the* symptom that tells us exactly why church isn't more. We're well familiar with the problem of church mean-

---

1. Various attributions include Sam Pascoe, Dr. Richard C. Halverson, and Leonard Ravenhill.

ing either the building or the event, seen in phrases like "I have to stop by the church" or "I can't go tomorrow; I have church."

But there's a third sense in which church is often used, one which receives far less scrutiny. In most cases today, churches exist organiza-tionally—like a business. "The church is having a Gospel meeting next week." "The church has a food pantry for the home-less." We speak about churches much the same way we speak about gyms, libraries, or even restaurants.

Since it's a business, the people involved fall into one of two catego-ries. Some folks are on that provider side of the counter, deciding what the church will look like. The pressure is placed on elders and ministers to put on the kind of worship, sermons, programs, and activities that will make people want to choose "our church" and get more and more involved once they join "us." There's a multimillion dollar industry built around helping churches know how to get this just right—what to put on the sign, how to use your building to your advantage, how long the sermon should be, how many songs to include and what type of songs they should be, what to train your greeters to say, what programs will bring people in, etc.

The rest are on the other side of the counter, the customer side, choosing which church they attend based on various criteria and choos-ing the level of involvement with which they're comfortable. They are all individuals who have their own walk with God, looking for the place that will help them (and possibly their family) strengthen that walk with God so they can go to Heaven.

The leadership's hope is that they develop enough of a brand loyalty among people that they will stay and get involved. Some of them may even stay around long enough and get involved enough to migrate to the "provider" side of the counter.

There's a sense of "*we* are here to help *you*." But who is the *we*? And who is the *you*? Don't the *you* have a responsibility to the *we*? And is it Biblical to have that split?

Such a distinction is not Biblical in any sense whatsoever. Though we generally use "church" to mean either the building, the event, or the organization, the Bible never uses the word in any of these senses. The church is a family, a temple made up of living stones, a body held together by what every joint supplies. Businesslike churches are based on precisely the opposite idea, and it shows in a number of ways.

Businesslike churches are reliant on paid staff.

This isn't an anti-paid staff point, as Paul laid out plainly that paying full-time ministry workers is good and acceptable (1 Corinthians 9:14). Seeing as I'm currently somebody who works in a paid ministry job, please don't misconstrue this point as being anti-paid ministry. However, talk to any minister and you'll find we've almost all had the "that's the preacher's job" experience. In many congregations if somebody wasn't being paid to evangelize, visit the sick, call on the absent, and reach out to visitors, some of those things simply wouldn't happen.

As I was hitting a bit of a writer's block looking for ways to articulate this point, I found myself on Facebook. (How do we always end up there?) Right at the top of my feed I stumbled across the perfect illustration for this point. It came in the form of a humorous video of a man doing one of those TV show obstacle courses, with the twist being that they had added labels to each of the obstacles depicting different ministry challenges and expectations. A sampling of some of the labels: visionary leadership, people leaving the church, angry old lady mad about the song service, building projects, people treating me weird because I'm a minister, making time for my family, no private life (the "glass house" effect).

Though their intended message was something along the lines of "Ministry is hard but God gets us through it," they inadvertently made this point for me better than I ever could. The minister is expected to grow the church numerically, help coordinate improvements to the building, and respond to and appease all of the complaints from the "customers" so they don't leave. At the same time there is the awkward position of being a part of a church family, but a hired part, leading to him and his family being treated differently and friendships that are often tenuous at best.

The businesslike church almost asks for this kind of attitude though. It excuses people from fulfilling a number of their commanded Biblical duties with the excuse that they're all very busy and the minister just has more time for it. And, unfortunately, ministers can further the problem too.

It's easy to have the attitude of "I have the education, the training, and the experience" and become selfish with the pulpit or assume that people can't handle deep theological teaching. It's also easy to elevate our work as being the biggest factor of a church's success. You don't have to look far to see quotes like, "The best way to revive a church is to build a fire in the pulpit" (allegedly by D.L. Moody). And, it's incredibly easy to have the attitude that little should be expected of the members. That's why you'll hear quotes like these from time to time: "Most people have had a hard week. Take it easy on them from the pulpit." "People are busy. We can't expect them to give more than 2 hours per week to the church."

There's a level of pride involved when we expect so little of the people in the pews. We're essentially saying "It's not fair to expect everyone to be as interested in God as I am." How easily we forget that it isn't our talents, knowledge, or personality that make the church go. As we'll see later, the Scriptures present the church as the spiritual equivalent of a potluck meal, with everyone being tasked to provide for each other. From both sides of the counter, the prevailing model of church today puts far too much emphasis on the staff, turning us into a restaurant rather than a potluck.

Businesslike churches are reliant on lectures.

About 3 years in to my first ministry work I attended a conference for preachers. It was one I had attended before, and I benefited greatly from it each time I went... but this particular occasion was different. At the time I was going through a lot in my ministry, facing a number of personal challenges and difficulties within the church.

As much as I learned from the lessons, I kept finding myself thinking I'd trade all of the conferences and lectures in the world just to get to sit and talk to an older minister and pick his brain about my problems. I had so many questions that I just couldn't answer in my inexperience, and I needed somebody who could answer them. That's nothing against the good, talented brothers who were speaking at the conference. It's just an inescapable fact that a message preached to a room of people can't address the questions and struggles of each individual listener.

As I lamented my lack of place to turn to really connect those lessons to my life, it hit me: As a preacher, this is the challenge the members who hear my sermons face every single week. Yes, people can grow through sermons and Bible classes, but one-size-fits-all instruction couldn't possibly ever reach every person where they are, teach them at their level, address any questions they have, and give them practical ways to apply it in their walk.

The solution for me was the same solution we must offer everybody else. I went home from that conference and prayed that God would place a mentor in my life, somebody I could ask about these difficulties and who could share experienced, Biblical advice. Of course, that's exactly what He did. A brother who preached at a congregation a few minutes down the road took me under his wing, and I'm not sure where I would have been without him.

That kind of mentorship and guidance was what I needed to grow and serve God. There was no other way to get knowledge that was specific to my particular difficulties. I don't think it's a stretch to say that that's what every Christian needs in their walk with God, yet most of them will rarely have such a relationship, if ever.

Beyond that, it takes years and years and years of sermons and Bible classes to give people even an elementary education in the Scriptures. This is because there's just not enough time, and because listening to lectures with little to no interaction is literally the worst way to learn for retention. And yet we keep feeding them sermons and Bible classes and wondering why they aren't growing, why we aren't evangelizing, why they persist in the same sins and misunderstandings year after year.

In both *Pagan Christianity?* by Frank Viola and George Barna and *Total Church* by Tim Chester and Steve Timmis, the argument is made that the singular monologue version of sermon we have today looks nothing like what the original church relied on for their teaching. Both books make the argument that the way we do preaching today is actually a result of Constantine's secularization of the church, where Roman citizens were encouraged and even pressured by the Roman government to join the Christian church. At that point churches adapted their practice. Rather than being an inter-connected family, they had people among them they knew they wouldn't see throughout the week, so they loaded up their teaching into one message to try and get them all the learning they needed. We're stuck with their compromising, far less effective formula to this day.

We have to wake up to the lesson all these centuries have taught us—there's just no way that sermons and Bible classes can be personalized enough to give all of the correction, encouragement, and instruction each needs, there's no way they can cover all the topics people need to know, and there's no way people can retain enough to be meaningfully molded into Christlikeness from such small spiritual meals. And yet that's the diet the average Christian receives as a part of their church life. In short, we typically expect way, way too much to come from sermons and classes.

The businesslike approach to church creates customers who can only give a few hours per week and who can only consume, which places the onus on the providers to keep serving up these spiritual meals for the customers. Customers then choose the church where the preaching and teaching best meet their needs and the style they prefer.

Businesslike churches are reliant on marketing.

What steps would you need to take if you wanted to open a restaurant? Aside from all the paperwork and red tape, the list includes things like finding a location, putting out signage so people know you're there, advertising your menu items, offering special deals and coupons, and ultimately providing the kind of food and environment that would make people want to come back.

How do churches reach people today? The list includes finding and/or developing a location for a building, putting up a sign with the website and times, advertising what kind of church you are (experiential, Bible-teaching, family-oriented, etc.), offering special events, and ultimately providing the kind of worship, preaching, and environment that would make people want to come back.[2] We try to get them in the door, and once they come in we want them to like our singing, our preacher's sermons, our youth group, our building, etc. Essentially, we're selling ourselves to customers.

The more people we have in a congregation who came in under those terms, the greater the provider/consumer divide in the church grows. And, what is the centerpiece of church marketing? The program.

Businesslike churches are reliant on programs.

Just like the restaurant that rises or falls based on what they offer on the menu, so churches today have come to rise or fall based on what they offer on their menu of activities and programs. I don't know how many people have told me that in order for our church family to grow we're going to need families with kids so we can have a children's/youth program. I'm obviously not averse to having families with young children attending our congregation, but where on earth do we get the idea that a church is dead unless they can offer people a good youth program? Certainly not from the Bible.

More and more, though, small churches continue to be held down and passed over while the larger churches add more and more programs to segment their congregation all the more so that every demographic has a catered experience—children's ministry, youth ministry, college

---

2. Once again, let me offer the disclaimer that I'm not saying it's wrong to have a sign, a building, a website, or any of these things. However, the over-reliance on them as outreach and church growth strategies makes for a strong parallel to what businesses do.

ministry, singles/young professional ministry, young families ministry, divorced ministry, seniors ministry.

I once heard a preacher from one of these large congregations speak on church growth based on the Acts 2 church. He did a great job of exegeting the text, outlining all of the elements that made the church go in its early days—elements like fellowship, worship, and study.

It was when he got to the application that the lesson took a turn. He shared how his church had applied all of these elements: "They fellowshipped, so we started a regular potluck program. They studied the apostles' teaching, so we've invested heavily in having a good Bible class program. They were generous with their possessions, so we have a benevolence program…" and so on.

When I read Acts 2, I don't see an organization putting on programs that people can participate in. I see a family of Spirit-filled people doing all of these things naturally because it's what Jesus-following people do, not because the Apostles scheduled it into their lives.

Much like the point about paid ministry staff, the point here is not to paint programs as sinful or anti-Biblical. The point is to get us asking the questions: How would a business operate, how would a family operate, and which one do we most resemble?

Most important of course, is to ask ourselves which model most closely aligns with the Bible. Does trying to determine what people want and offering it to them in hopes that they'll feel prioritized align with dying to self and following Jesus at all costs? Though there certainly are preachers, elders, and teachers in the Bible, was there ever a sense of church being a *we* putting church on for a *you*?

SYMPTOMS

If this theory is correct, that the consumer/provider split is hurting the church and keeping it from being all it can be, and if we really have placed too much weight on the providers staff, sermons, marketing, and programs, one would expect to see certain signs.

Paid Staffers

If it's true Christians are overly reliant on their church staff to do God's work, you would expect to have a church culture where there are many inactive, ineffective, disengaged Christians.

As long as I can remember I've heard church leaders echo the common 90/10 principle, that 90% of the work in volunteer organizations is done by 10% of the people. Many congregations have resigned themselves to this principle. Many are fighting against it, trying to bump that 10% up to 20 or 30. Talk to any group of ministers and you'll hear complaints about how it's like pulling teeth to get people to join in evangelistic efforts or to sign up to teach Bible classes. Look around your congregation this Sunday. What percentage of the people are taking an active role in ministering to their fellow Christians? What about you? How are you serving, teaching, loving, caring, and/or encouraging week in and week out? I'm not talking about attending things that have been put on for you by a provider. No, I'm talking about taking initiative on themselves to minister.

There may be congregations where that percentage is much higher than others, even better than 50%, but from my own experiences, from my discussions with other ministers, from what books and studies and sermons have all told us for years, those would be the exceedingly rare exception.

On the other side of the coin, over-reliance on staff would also make burnout among those staff members a fair expectation, and once again that's exactly what we often see. Every year ministers get chewed up and spit out by congregations. Plenty of ministers struggle with depression and anxiety, made worse by the fairly common belief that those who are in ministry and supposedly closest to God shouldn't ever face those struggles. In a system where ministers have to project themselves as flawless or risk losing their jobs, and in a system where ministers are expected to give and give and give and go find their spiritual and emotional nourishment elsewhere, it's no wonder we see burnout.

Finally, if our church system is too reliant on the staff, you would expect to see a minister celebrity culture. The best, most talented ministers would end up at the biggest congregations, drawing more people in for the good preaching and vision. People would seek out sermons from their favorite preachers online and feel more encouraged from those than from anything their local congregation offers. People would flock to conventions with posters that share an odd resemblance with those of music festivals, listing all the big names people will want to travel to hear. What do we see? All of the above.

Are we too reliant on the staff? The eye test says yes.

Preaching

What would you expect to see if it's true that congregations are too reliant on sermons? You would expect to see Biblical illiteracy. If somewhere between thirty minutes and three hours is all the teaching a person is exposed to each week, and it's done in the one-size-fits-all manner of sermons and Bible classes, it would be difficult for them to grow to Christian maturity and to know their Bible well.

Barna Group research documents this for us. They set out to determine how many people who claimed to be Christians held a Biblical worldview. The definition Barna used included holding to six basic tenets, believing that believing that "absolute moral truth exists; the Bible is totally accurate in all of the principles it teaches; Satan is considered to be a real being or force, not merely symbolic; a person cannot earn their way into Heaven by trying to be good or do good works; Jesus Christ lived a sinless life on earth; and God is the all-knowing, all-powerful creator of the world who still rules the universe today. Only 17% of churchgoers agreed with all six of those in Barna's 2015 study.[3]

Additionally, in a 2001 book titled *Boiling Point: How Coming Cultural Shifts Will Change Your Life*, George Barna and Mark Hatch shared that 81% of professing Christians in one survey thought "God helps

---

3. "Competing Worldviews Influence Today's Christians," Barna Group, https://www.barna.com/research/competing-worldviews-influence-todays-christians/ May 9, 2017.

those who help themselves" was a Bible verse.[4] Only 17% of churchgoers in a 2018 Barna Group study could explain what the phrase "Great Commission" means.[5] In a time where the Bible is with us more than ever via the smartphone, American Christians know the Bible less than ever.

How many in your congregation can list the 10 commandments or the Beatitudes? How many engage in the regular discipline of memory work? How many can answer the difficult questions put forth by today's atheists? Conversely, how many would say they want to study the Bible better but don't know how to do so?

We're just talking about the basics at this point. This does not begin to scratch the surface of what is needed to be holy people, imitating Jesus Christ and becoming more and more like Him every day. How on earth is that going to happen if people are so Biblically illiterate and remain spiritually immature?

And, once again you'd expect to see the proliferation of premium preaching—the podcasts, the big events, the YouTube videos—revealing an underlying belief that what we need is more, better, one-off lessons from talented speakers rather than slow, steady, personalized teaching. And, once again, we're seeing that more than ever with the event calendar being jam-packed year-round.

Marketing

If businesslike marketing truly were a problem in the modern church system, we would expect to see a number of churches opt for crowd-pleasing doctrinal errors.

Just like the restaurant that is advertising their food to people has to consider what the customers want and prepare accordingly, business-minded churches are prone to all sorts of compromise as they try to keep up with the congregations around them for the attention and attendance of the community.

4. George Barna and Mark Hatch, "Boiling Point: How Coming Cultural Shifts will Change Your Life." Regal Books, 2001, 90.

5. "51% of Churchgoers Don't Know of the Great Commission," Barna Group, barna.com/research/half-churchgoers-not-heard-great-commission/ March 27, 2018.

It's hard to compete with the entertaining, energetic worship being put on by other congregations in town, and people aren't as interested in sound, Bible-based doctrine as much as they are in hearing sermons centered on them and how God is going to fulfill all their hopes and dreams. The marketing approach of selling ourselves rather than Christ and the Good News has lead plenty of congregations to go all-in on entertainment and feel good preaching rather than humble worship and God-glorifying, Bible-driven preaching.

Additionally, if churches are too reliant on businesslike marketing, you would expect to see a lack of enthusiasm for evangelism. The church exploded onto the scene in Acts without a building, a sign, a website, flyers, or anything else we rely on today. It's exciting to try to lead people to Jesus. It's far less exciting to try to get people to come to our church, particularly if as a customer one doesn't feel a particularly strong attachment to the church anyway. As Christianity wanes in our country generation after generation, and as younger generations grow disillusioned about evangelism, we're seeing the effects of church marketing vs. Gospel sharing.

Finally, if marketing were an issue, you would see Christians who act like customers. In a world of Yelp reviews and a "customer is always right" economy, customers are more empowered than ever to speak their mind and push for their own way. It's no surprise that there are plenty of these folks in our churches. It might be that they don't like the song selection, that the sermon was too long, that the proverbial carpet color of their choice wasn't chosen, or that they weren't specifically catered to in some way. So, they complain, cause division through rumors and gossip, and threaten to leave, because the customer is always right. After all, they contribute and add to the church's attendance numbers, in essence saying, "I don't need you—you need me." Because the church's marketing told them that.

I'm not claiming every Christian is like this, or even most. But there are plenty of them out there, and they've been created by a church culture that tells them it's all about them. Church leaders cannot continue to be surprised when the people they attract as customers come in and act like customers.

Programs

If churches are too reliant on programs, you would expect to see a number of effects, starting with the rise of megachurches. More than just about anything, if the modern church system were overly reliant on programs, one would surely expect to see the rise of bigger churches and the slow demise of small churches. Two out of three churches with under 100 in attendance are in decline,[6] while most churches with an attendance over 250 are growing.[7] Church customers are abandoning the congregations that have less to offer and flocking to the ones that have all the programs they might want.

Coupled closely with this is the practice of church shopping, where people choose congregations based on what the congregation offers them rather than on the opportunity to serve and grow close with a spiritual family. And, closely related to church shopping is the issue of church hopping. I chose the phone plan I'm on because they offered me a shiny, new smartphone for free if I signed up. At the end of my contract I'm sure I'll switch to another company when they offer me a shinier, newer smartphone. I'll keep bouncing around like that until I die, because I'm a customer looking for the best deal for me.

If you are under the impression that church is all about you and what they can offer you in your personal walk with God, of course you'll go where you most want to be. Can't get along with a fellow member? There aren't enough activities or kids for your family? They brought in a new preacher you don't like as much? What do you do? You start looking for somewhere else to go. In most areas in America big enough to house two or more churches of a certain type, people just move on to the church a

---

6. Thom Rainer, "Is There a Church Death Spiral?" ThomRainer.com, https://thomrainer.com/2017/07/church-death-spiral/, July 3, 2017.

7. Aaron Earls, "Big Get Bigger While the Small Get Smaller," Christianity Today, https://www.christianitytoday.com/news/2019/march/lifeway-research-church-growth-attendance-size.html, March 06, 2019.

few miles down the road, dropping the old one like an expired cell phone plan.

If it's true that we're over-reliant on programs in this organizational, businesslike approach to church, one would expect to see a number of Christians living with a checklist mentality. It's vitally important to understand this principle: What we win them with is what we win them to. If we didn't get them in the door with the truth of Jesus and the dedication to following Him, we can't suddenly expect them to operate as though that's the deal. If they were won with programs aimed right at them, they are going to expect a church life continually aimed at them. Sacrificing for others, giving up more time, and being a functioning part of the church weren't part of the deal. Put on the service for them, offer them their programs, and they'll do their job of showing up and dropping money in the plate. Ask anything else, change anything up, or cater to somebody else first, and they're gone.

And, finally, if our businesslike church culture were too reliant on programs, we would also see a heavily individualized Christianity, because if people are choosing and attending their congregation because of what it offers them, it's only natural that they would view their Christianity as an individual pursuit.

Take a look at Christianity from a bird's eye view and you'll see that it's extremely deep-seated in us to think of our Christianity as a private walk. Most of the Christian living books you will ever read have a "you and God" focus. While it's certainly of the utmost importance that we each walk with God each day and grow in our individual relationships with Him, Christianity is not a private pursuit. We are not a bunch of disconnected individuals, all trying to go to Heaven in our own walks, brought together to the church that will help us do so.

How many in a given congregation are seeing each other away from the building between the Sundays? How many are opening their homes to their fellow Christians? How many are gathering to pray and pore over the Bible with another Christian every week? How many are ministering to others? Once again, in most congregations, that number would be quite low. The power in our congregations is in our unity, in the Spirit working through all of us together.

Why isn't church more? Perhaps because the church isn't really a church. When it's run like a business by providers and for consumers, it's not a family where everybody provides for each other and looks out for each other. It's not the body God intended it to be where every system, bone, and muscle helps the other do its job. Until we break out of the provider/consumer paradigm, wipe the slate clean, and get back to the image of church that the Holy Spirit painted for us, church can't ever be more.

DISCUSSION QUESTIONS

1. What does the Biblical concept of "church" mean? What are ways we use the word? How do the two differ?

2. Would you consider yourself to be on the producer side or the consumer side of the church?

3. What can you do to lessen the divide between those two sides?

CHURCH RESET

Virtually every church is faithful at Sunday services—
and putting much time, energy, and money into them.
But statistically, most churches are not doing a great job
at making disciples who make disciples.

Preston Sprinkle[1]

MAYBE THE BUSINESS model is normal. Maybe the side effects discussed in the last chapter are just an unavoidable truth of the modern
world. Maybe God doesn't really care about how we organize a church,
but just about what what we teach and do.

Providentially, we actually know exactly how Jesus would respond in
such a situation. In John 6 we see the account of Jesus feeding 5,000 men.
Their instant reaction was to declare that He truly was the prophet they
had been anticipating and was the one they wanted as their king. Even as
He got away with His apostles and crossed the sea, they still pursued Him.

---

1. Preston Sprinkle, *Go: Returning Discipleship to the Front Lines of Faith*, Colo-
rado Springs: NavPress, 2016. 153.

Isn't that exactly what we'd want? Thousands of people who believe in Jesus and are ready to follow Him, even making Him their king? Even the greatest of our seeker-sensitive, producer/consumer churches couldn't dream of starting with a dedicated following 5,000 strong. If Jesus believed in our business-like approach, He would have been well on His way. He would've kept the meals coming, even offering variety because, like Israel in the desert, people aren't going to stay on board for a steady diet of the same meals that brought them in. He would have set the apostles about the business of making sure each demographic was being kept content and connected. In short, He would have done whatever it took to keep those numbers up and offered them whatever they needed to stay.

And yet, despite this situation that many church leaders would give their right arm to have, Jesus did the unthinkable. First, He ran away and left the crowd behind (6:15). Then, when they persisted in following Him, He told them straight to their faces that they only wanted Him for the free meal He provided (6:26). Finally, when the people refused to pick up on the hint that He didn't want them following Him because they didn't accept Him as He was, He went for the one of the most strange-sounding teachings He could give. "Then Jesus said to them, "Most assuredly, I say to you, unless you eat the flesh of the Son of Man and drink His blood, you have no life in you" (6:53).

The crowd struggled greatly with this teaching (6:52, 60). You can almost picture the perplexed looks on their faces—"He wants us to do *what*?" The result? "From that time many of His disciples went back and walked with Him no more" (6:66). All of those followers… gone. Even after His greatest miracle of rising from the tomb we see only 120 gathered in the upper room in Acts 1. He turned a following of 5,000 into a following of 120. At His ascension He left behind a group that was 1/40th the size it had once been. Not exactly a great church growth strategy, right?

Did He really have to send them away though? Sure, they were following Him for the wrong reasons, but maybe over time they would have come around if He could have just kept offering the right things to keep them coming. Likewise, people who come to our churches because we have advertising that speaks to them and their wants might not be coming for Jesus, but maybe if we keep them coming, we can turn them into real followers eventually. Thankfully, Jesus did not and does not think like us.

Jesus knew that if they didn't accept Him as Lord it didn't matter how dedicated they were; they were unfit to carry out His purpose. It's the same reason why He turned away the would-be followers who wanted to say farewell or bury their dead in Luke 9:57-62. It's the same reason why He turned away the rich young ruler despite the man's supposedly impeccable dedication to law-keeping. If people didn't value Him above all else, He knew they weren't fit for discipleship.

That's why the people He ended up making His followers were those who dropped their nets and left their boats or hopped up and left the tax booth behind. He meant what He said when He told the disciples, "If anyone desires to come after Me, let him deny himself, and take up his cross daily, and follow Me" (Luke 9:23). Jesus didn't want customers who liked Him for what He had to offer them. He wanted disciples who were ready to take up their crosses for Him.

Why did Jesus demand so much more commitment than we do? Because He wasn't here to amass a crowd. He was here to train people to be like Him in order to launch the kingdom, a worldwide project predicated on preparing people and sending them rather than attracting people and keeping them. He knew that unless people were following Him as both their Savior *and* Lord of their entire lives, they weren't fit for carrying out the goals of the kingdom. With such a lofty, worldwide purpose in mind, His method was to establish a church to carry it out. Why would He want a church system that turned around and viewed crowds and success exactly the opposite of the way He did?

The answer? He didn't. What we see today is largely the antithesis of everything He intended His church to be and bears little resemblance to what He put in place through the apostles and the Holy Spirit. Why isn't church more? Because it's not operating the way Jesus intended.

If the producer/consumer model isn't what Jesus had in mind, and if it is what's holding us back from seeing a church that is more, what's the alternative?

As with anything in Christianity, the answer is to go back to the Bible. However, being a Biblical church isn't just about espousing Biblical teachings from the pulpit and observing Biblical principles for worship and leadership structure. It's about how we do the things we do, how we organize, how we mobilize. Though our base doctrines may be perfectly Biblical and our worship may be exactly what God wants, the business-like, consumer-provider model of church activity just can't be found in the Scriptures. We have built the best church that marketing professionals can design and it's left us wanting. Maybe it's time to give the Holy Spirit another shot at it.

So what does the New Testament tell us about the church? What kind of picture is painted there? Let's look at a few of the key Scriptures that give us an idea of what Christ had in mind for His bride.

THE PRIESTHOOD

"The priesthood of all believers" is a belief that's been shared throughout Christendom for 500 years since the Reformers began to throw off the shackles of the Roman Catholic system that required a middleman between Christians and their God. With roots in Isaiah, the idea is spelled out most clearly in 1 Peter 2. There Peter tells us that we are "living stones" being built on the foundation of Christ into a spiritual house and a holy priesthood (2:4) so we can offer spiritual sacrifices to God. He repeats this thought in 2:9, calling his recipients a royal priesthood chosen to proclaim the praises of God.

Though not using the term for priesthood, Ephesians 2:19-22 carries a similar concept to what Peter used regarding each of us functioning as stones who are being built together into a home of God in the Spirit. Romans 12:1 also hints at our priesthood in urging us to present ourselves as living and holy sacrifices. Not coincidentally, the discussion in that chapter immediately turns to serving the church (the people, not the organization), which in turn closely parallels the wording used in 1 Corinthians 12 and Ephesians 4 which we'll examine later in this chapter.

As always, the inspired writers used the words they used for a reason. Priest isn't just a throwaway term. If we are all priests, it's implied that carrying on our own private walk with God isn't enough. It's also implied that we all have duties to fulfill in God's spiritual house, the body of believers we call the church. In the Law there was no place for a priest who only showed up for holy days and then went home and lived the same as everybody else. It was not enough for a priest to merely practice personal holiness.

Ask yourself: Does church today look more like a priesthood of all believers, or like the model Israel had where the majority of the people went about living their own lives while a small group did the work of priests? Don't take that as saying there are no elements of the priesthood of all believers in modern Christianity at all. Instead, I simply mean the question as it is stated: If you had to pick which model we most resemble, which would it be?

Anywhere the 90/10 principle (or anything remotely near it) is in effect, the question has already been answered. Anywhere evangelism is lagging because "that's the preacher's job," the question has already been answered. Anywhere Christians go all week without seeing or talking to each other outside of the building, the question has already been answered.

To get back to the Bible we have to go beyond giving lip service to the concept of the priesthood of all believers and start acting on it. If you are a Christian, you are a priest. Whether you're a new Christian or an old one, a minister, elder, deacon, teacher, or none of the above, a male or a female, you are a priest. You've been set apart by God for service in His house, the church. You aren't just a priest, though. You're a body part, too.

THE BODY

1 Corinthians 12

In 1 Corinthians 12 Paul answered a question (unseen by us) the Corinthian Christians had asked him about spiritual gifts. While spiritual gifts can be a touchy subject, there is still an important principle to be found in this chapter. That principle: that God's church is a body of which each person is a part, and He has given each part a role to play. 1 Corinthians 12:7 is the key: "But the manifestation of the Spirit is given to each one for the profit of all." Two thoughts stand out in contrast to consumeristic Christianity.

First, every person has a part to play. "If the foot should say, "Because I am not a hand, I am not of the body," is it therefore not of the body? And if the ear should say, "Because I am not an eye, I am not of the body," is it therefore not of the body?" (1 Corinthians 12:15-16). Medically, it's a problem when a body has an ear that doesn't hear, or a hand that can't grab, or a foot than can't walk. The same is true of the church. The more members we have who aren't contributing anything other than their attendance and some money, the unhealthier the body is. The more people we have who say "I'm too busy right now" or "That's the preacher's job," the weaker the church will be.

You are not at your strongest until you're exercising your gift for the good of the church. It's true that the church is for the individual, to help him or her grow and stay grounded. But God intended the individual for the church, too. The converts in Acts 2 were immediately added to the church. Paul often transitions from his doctrinal teaching sessions about how God saves us in Christ right into how we can love and serve one another (see Romans 12, Ephesians 4, Colossians 3) because loving and serving one's church family is the true sign of a Christian (John 13). A Christian's growth is stunted so long as they are not regularly serving their church family.

We understand this concept with the human's need for God. As Augustine said, "You made us for yourself and our hearts find no peace until they rest in you." Similarly, CS Lewis wrote "A car is made to run on petrol, and it would not run properly on anything else. Now God designed the human machine to run on Himself." Both were making the case that the human heart was made for God and can never be complete without Him. Similarly, the Christian is a creature that will always be lacking until they are growing in the Spirit to serve their Christian family.

Second, the prominent must give way to the less prominent.

> And the eye cannot say to the hand, "I have no need of you"; nor again the head to the feet, "I have no need of you." No, much rather, those members of the body which seem to be weaker are necessary. And those members of the body which we think to be less honorable, on these we bestow greater honor; and our unpresentable parts have greater modesty, but our presentable parts have no need. But God composed the body, having given greater honor to that part which lacks it, that there should be no schism in the body, but that the members should have the same care for one another.
>
> 1 Corinthians 12:21-25

Businesslike churches gather around the minister. Biblical churches realize that, counter to our human tendency to gather around the most talented or educated, we must gather around the Spirit by downplaying the minister and raising up those we'd least expect.

As discussed in the previous chapter, many churches today rise and fall on the talents of their leadership. The Bible makes it clear for us time and time again that God has no need for super-talented individuals to accomplish His purposes. He needs the submissive, the faithful. He delights in using the weak to show His strength. That's why He pared Gideon's army down to 300, why He chose David over His more physically qualified brothers, why He took on fishermen and a tax collector to start His church.

In order to make this happen in our churches, the prominent have to acknowledge what the less notable members bring to the table. Then, the prominent must step back and create room for the less notable to contribute. Telling them that their job is to attend on Sunday because it's an encouragement to the rest of us does not count. Perfect attendance is not a spiritual gift. God gives each and every one of us the Spirit for serving the people around us in some way. Until we have a system that disciples people and helps them find their role in the building up of the body, we are saying to the hand, "I have no need of you."

We often lament the inactivity and lack of commitment of so many Christians. Have we ever considered that it might be because we aren't expecting anything of them? Because we aren't training them outside of sermons? Because we aren't giving them anything to do? Similarly, we lament the oft-heard slogan of the deserter, "I have my own relationship with God; I don't need the church." Should we really be surprised, though? Wouldn't that be the natural side effect of a church culture built to cater to individual, consumeristic Christians?

That's what separates Biblical leadership from businesslike leadership. Preaching and teaching are most certainly gifts, and important ones at that. The thing that keeps those gifts from turning into a consumer/provider setup is whether everyone else is being equipped and launched to exercise their gifts as well.

As a preacher, I often catch myself just hoping those on the fringes will keep on coming. I think it's my job to preach in such a way that they can get something from the message and hopefully hold on to their Christianity enough to show up most Sundays and maybe even increase their commitment. What this passage and Ephesians 4 teach is that *I* need *them*. Admittedly, as a preacher, I don't often believe that.

There are some people we may look at and think "They're never going to contribute much." When we do so, we're judging by man's standards and we're forgetting that the power to do anything is not in us. When I have that attitude, I'm saying I can contribute to the church more than they can because of my perceived superior intelligence or talents or goodness. A cross-centered, sin-examining look at myself would instead lead me to say, "If God can cleanse *me* and use *me* for service, He can use *anybody*."

Ephesians 4

Some may want to dismiss 1 Corinthians 12 from the conversation due to its focus on spiritual gifts, but the same principle of the church as a body is repeated in Ephesians 4 in a way that shows it is not dependent on miraculous spiritual gifts for their validity. Paul started Ephesians introducing important doctrinal points such as the supremacy in Christ, our blessings in Christ, how we were made alive in Christ, and the union of Jew and Gentile in the church. After setting forth those doctrinal truths in chapters 1-3, he turned his attention to the more practical matters of church life and Christian behavior.

In His outline of how the church should function, Paul starts by emphasizing the God-given leadership roles. The section starting in 4:11 first gives its attention to those who have been gifted to lead—apostles, prophets, evangelists, pastors, and teachers (NKJV). If he intended the more specific uses of apostles and prophets (the twelve, and people with direct messages from God)—which I'm inclined to believe he did—that leaves us with evangelists, pastors, and teachers today. Evangelists, of course, are proclaimers of the Good News. Pastors simply refers to shepherds, people tasked with guarding the flock. Teachers are those who help us understand the Word. So, to this point in Ephesians 4 we have the exhortation to be unified, the reminder that in Christ's victory He has given gifts to men in different measures, and the explanation that those gifts are manifested first of all in these roles.

Much like in 1 Corinthians 12, the key difference that keeps this from being a foundation for the consumer-provider model is in the purpose for the leader's role. Consumerism sees evangelists, shepherds, and teachers as providers, people who put on "church" for the customers to come and take in so they can have better individual Christian lives. Paul's progression in this passage paints a much different picture.

Second, after outlining the leadership roles, Paul provided the purpose for which they were given. Why did God create these leadership roles, then? "For the equipping of the saints for the work of ministry, for the building up of the body of Christ" (4:12). These people have been given their role by God not merely to serve others, but to serve others and equip others to turn and serve others. As we examined in the last chapter, this is not how things typically go. Church is "choose your own adventure" for most Christians. If they want to be highly involved with the work of the church, or if they want to really grow in their personal study, then that's what they'll do. If they don't, we just hope they'll come around. We invite them to the next event or preach sermons about commitment and the importance of attendance, and it's up to them to step up.

What Paul outlines here is quite the opposite. This is not "choose your own adventure." It's "be trained until you're strong enough to exercise the gifts God has given you to the good of the people around you." Church leadership is in place to equip every member to do ministry work. Just as it was with the priesthood, in God's eyes every Christian is a minister as well.

No, I'm not naive enough to think that every member of every church is going to join in. The goal, though, should be to create a culture where people know what they're signing up for. In my experience, it's usually those who are passionate for the Lord and looking to keep the fire going throughout the week who are out of place in many congregations. As I'm writing this book I keep hearing from Christians who feel like they have no place to turn because no one else in their congregation is interested in fellowship outside of set "church times," because evangelistic zeal is lacking, because nobody's interested in gathering around the Word outside of Bible class and the sermon.

If we're equipping and sending, that culture shifts. People understand that if you're a part of this church, you're going to be trained to minister to those around you. The lazy and disinterested will be made uncomfortable, drawn to either change or leave. Isn't that how Jesus did it? He placed that choice before people who wanted to follow Him—either decide you're all in, or go do something else.

Preachers, elders, and teachers—we have to look at ourselves as the key in the ignition. We've been put in place by God to start a cycle that will sustain itself if we do it right. Members, it's your role to put yourself in place to be trained by your spiritual leaders to then turn and serve the people around you.

Third, after listing the offices of the leadership and explaining their role, Paul provides the goal they are to pursue in Ephesians 4:13: "...till we *all* come to the unity of the faith and of the knowledge of the Son of God, to a perfect man, to the measure of the stature of the fullness of Christ" (emp. added). The goal is maturity. What does maturity look like? It looks like Jesus Christ. How will that play out in practical terms? How will we know someone is reaching maturity?

First, they join in the unity of the faith, being interconnected with their church family. Many think it's a sign of their superior spirituality that they can withdraw from the church and "come to God in their own way," as the saying goes. On the contrary, that's one of the surest signs they are greatly lacking in maturity.

Secondly with regard to maturity, they have a knowledge of the Son of God, understanding how Jesus would act in a given situation, submitting to the Father as He did, and desiring what He desires. My favorite illustration for Christian maturity is that of a human's progression with food. A newborn can't handle anything beyond milk, and they need it served to them straight from the breast or the bottle. So the new Christian needs the basic milk of the Word, and they need it served to them in the very limited ways in which they can eat (Hebrews 5:12, 1 Peter 2:2). As the newborn grows, they can start digesting food that grows progressively more solid over time. So the young Christian can be spoon-fed progressively meatier truths by the spiritually mature in their lives.

Not long after, though, they learn to feed themselves the food that's given to them. They can handle a spoon, and then a fork. The new Christian must grow to the point where they can take the food that's been prepared for them in the form of sermons, Bible classes, articles, books, and the like, and use those to feed themselves.

Eventually the child will mature enough to prepare their own food, basic as it may be at first. Maybe they start by preparing a bowl of cereal, then a peanut butter and jelly sandwich, even scrambling an egg after a while. Eventually the newborn Christian should be led to develop their own food, being able to open up the Bible and glean something from it each time. Their study habits should develop to the point where they can use verses in context and grasp what's being discussed. Here's where the change must come, though. Many stop here and consider someone who knows the Word and has a strong personal spiritual life to be mature. Biblically, however, that's not where the journey ends.

Finally, as the child grows into their teenage years they grow to where they can prepare foods that can be served for others. They learn how to make a casserole. They learn the skill of preparing an entree and sides and get the hang of measuring ingredients. The more practice they get at that, the better the meals they will serve. So the final step in Christian maturity is to know the kitchen (study tools) and the food (the Bible, and by extension Christ Himself) well enough to be able to prepare a meal for others and regularly engage in feeding others. This doesn't necessarily mean preaching sermons or teaching Bible classes. Sometimes it just means something as simple as sitting across the table from a less mature Christian and helping them walk through the problems in their lives from a Gospel-centered perspective. It's walking with Christ so you can help show others how to walk with Christ, so they can show others how to walk with Christ.

Until people reach that kind of maturity where they are proficient with the Word and can spiritually nourish others, our job isn't done. The individual's maturity is the goal. Consumeristic churches count how many people they bring in. Biblical churches count how many people they bring to maturity in Christ. If you're a church leader, ask yourself—would I be content with bringing in good numbers even if those people aren't being brought to maturity?

One final point of emphasis in our section from Ephesians 4 is the purpose for each coming to maturity. Why is individual maturity the goal? First, because without it people are subject to every deceitful doctrine and the world's deception (4:14). The best way to keep Christians from backsliding is to help them reach maturity and start serving others.

But second, and most importantly in the context of the passage, the maturity of the individual is the goal because without it the whole body can't be all it's meant to be, and the growth of the whole body is also what's best for the individual. As we discussed with 1 Corinthians 12, few things strengthen our relationship with God like being used by Him to serve the people around us. Dying to self doesn't just mean giving up our pet sins, showing up to worship, and trying to have a daily devo time. It means putting ourselves in God's hands for His purposes. It's becoming submissive to Him in all things, just like Jesus. It's when we're serving in that role that He molds us, shapes us, and stretches us into what He needs us to be. We believe that the more we have of God, the better our lives will be, right? Then it's imperative that we pursue a vision of church that gives people this opportunity to have more of God.

We are to grow into Christ's headship (4:15), taking our orders from Him in the same way our bodies takes cues from our brains. When every one of us comes to that maturity in Christ, we are able to fulfill our role as effective members of the body.

Paul knew nothing of the 90/10 principle. His answer to the lack of engagement we see in so many of the Christians around us would not be to shrug his shoulders and hope the next sermon series will convict them to join in. His answer would be to let everyone know that they *will* be expected to minister and start equipping them to do so.

Take, for example, one preacher or shepherd who understands the duty God has given him in equipping others. He starts working to equip a select three or four to mature in Christ with the goal being that they can eventually to help others mature in Christ. Now you have four people in the congregation who are mature in Jesus. They in turn start helping others mature in Jesus. Before long you have a church full of people who are doing all the things Jesus would have us do—showing each other grace, bearing each other's burdens, serving each other, reaching the lost.

Beyond that, you stop having consumeristic people who hop from church to church because they're invested in the people around them. The burden on the preacher to keep everybody happy is lifted, because Jesus-like people know they aren't there to be served but to serve (Mark 10:45). "Family" would stop being a metaphor and start being a reality. The church wouldn't grow because people like what we offer them but because they're drawn to true, Gospel-driven love and unity, just as Jesus said they would be (John 17:20-23). Every joint supplies something and the church is built up as an immovable structure, centered on love and led by Jesus. When we ask the question, "Shouldn't church be more?" isn't this exactly what we mean?

THE END OF CONSUMERISM

This is why consumerism has to die. Despite whatever good intentions it may have, consumeristic Christianity keeps us from achieving this. When businesslike churches say things like "People only have so much time" or "We can't expect too much from people: they're really busy and life is hard," we think we're doing them a favor. What we don't realize is that by doing so we're hampering people's growth and limiting their walk with God. When businesslike churches depend on the ministry staff to bring people in and keep them coming, they rely on man's wisdom and talents rather than God working through everybody. How did we read the life of Jesus and get the idea that He would be reliant on the most talented and polished rather than the broken, the people we'd never expect to make a difference? When businesslike churches put all their eggs in the basket of sermons and group classes, they'll never see this version of church because people can't reach maturity by passively listening for an hour or two every week. When businesslike churches bring people in by figuring out what to offer and marketing it to them, they keep people from having all they can have in Jesus and keep themselves from receiving the blessing that others can offer in return when they grow to maturity. When businesslike churches keep people busy with specifically catered programs and activities, it tells them that church is about them and keeps them from the growth that comes from turning their Christianity outward.

Businesslike, consumeristic Christianity must go if we want a church that is more. Yet when I express these ideas some are quick to object that you can't say program-based, sermon-dependent churches are wrong—they're just one way of doing things, a way that has been developed to adapt to our modern world. The point is not that these things are wrong. The point is that by settling for convenience and familiarity and what we think works for people today, we're depriving ourselves and everyone around us of everything church could be.

The Spirit working in all of us is infinitely more powerful than talents exercised by a handful of us. By becoming businesslike and depending on preaching, staff, marketing, and programs, we're cutting off God's power source for the church. We're telling God (by implication) that we don't really need the Spirit because we've sharpened our speaking skills, studied all the best business practices, and read up on what people want in this day and age. We have crippled ourselves by our own design.

We've discussed that nagging feeling so many of us have that church can be more. This is it right here. The businesslike model shows us why church isn't more. Ephesians 4 shows us what church can be. There is a powerful, world-changing, life-giving version of church to be had if we go back to the Book.

Let's say the 90/10 principle is too pessimistic and it's closer to even 50% who are carrying out the work of the church. Can you imagine moving from that model to a model where nearly 100% are contributing week in and week out? How exciting is that? The only problem is, there's no quick fix. A church full of mature, Christ-following, family-serving disciples can't be manufactured overnight. We're going to have to put in the work.

Where do we start? Right where Jesus told us to.

DISCUSSION QUESTIONS

1. Taking what we learn from John 6, what would it look like if Jesus were to start a church today?

2. What does it mean that every Christian is a priest? How do you serve as a priest?

3. How does the picture of the body painted by Paul differ from what we see today?

4

JESUS IS THE MISSION

The Church exists for nothing else but to draw men into Christ, to make them little Christs. If they are not doing that, all the cathedrals, clergy, missions, sermons, even the Bible itself, are simply a waste of time. God became Man for no other purpose.

C.S. Lewis[1]

I WAS ONE OF THOSE people who hated math as a kid. Once you reached trigonometry, the amount of time it took to get through the problems felt like an eternity. Even worse, though, was when you would get an incorrect answer. In order to understand what went wrong you would have to go back and try to work it out again, step by step, until you could see where the deviation happened. In other words, it was one thing to know that an answer was incorrect. It was another to know why it was incorrect.

We have plenty of wrong answers for the purpose of church and the

1. C.S. Lewis, *Mere Christianity*, New York: HarperCollins, 2001 Edition. 199.

Christian life. Some are obvious, some are not. Before going back over the equation to see where we deviated, consider a few wrong answers.

Prosperity Gospel

No Bible-studying Christian takes the prosperity gospel (a.k.a. the "word of faith" movement or "health and wealth" doctrine) seriously. The idea that God wants to deliver us from sicknesses and poverty and any of life's other difficulties if we will merely "claim our success" or "rebuke our trials" is one that was foreign to Job...and Elijah...and Jeremiah... and Paul... and Peter...and, obviously, Jesus. It's a fleshly, short-sighted gospel that appeals to people's carnal instincts rather than calling them to deny self and follow Jesus.

Self-esteem

Closely related to the prosperity gospel is the self-esteem gospel. It's a lot easier to dress this up and make it sound biblical, but that doesn't make it true. Context-ripping of verses like Jeremiah 29:11 and Philippians 4:13 abound where this gospel is preached. This gospel avoids the uncomfortable truth that we are all unworthy of the salvation that's been given to us. It is determined to never let anybody feel bad. However, if we never feel godly sorrow, we can't repent. If we don't accept the biblical truth that Christ died for us when we were helpless, sinful enemies of God, we'll never have the humility that's required for change.

Social Justice

Social justice is a deeply biblical concept. Read the Old Testament prophets and you'll see that one of the biggest charges against Israel and Judah was their lack of working justice on behalf of the downtrodden and oppressed. Look at the promises of Christ's kingdom and you'll see that justice will abound. And, read Jesus' words at the end of Matthew 25 and you'll see that He will reject those disciples who neglect to care for the poor, the hungry, the sick, and so on.

However, social justice is not the Gospel. It is a byproduct of the Gospel, yes, but when a church puts all their focus on making the world a better place around them, things like doctrine, education, and evangelism often begin to fall through the cracks. If we feed the physically hungry but do nothing to feed the spiritually hungry, we are not being faithful as a church.

Morality

Like social justice, a moral, sin-forsaking life is a byproduct of the Christian life, and without it we cannot claim to be Christian. But living a moral life is not in itself the aim of Christianity. A person can never go clubbing, never sample drugs, never look at porn, never say a cuss word, and still be the furthest thing from a Christian. Just look at the rich young ruler. He claimed to have kept the commandments from his youth, but he left Jesus sorrowful because all of his morality still hadn't shattered the idol of his heart.

Phil Vischer, the creator of the popular VeggieTales cartoons for kids, came to this realization after the project had run its course. If you've seen any of their videos you'll remember how they taught children biblical principles like telling the truth and being kind along with recreating Bible stories with their cartoon vegetables. Vischer later realized that just because they were teaching ideas from the Bible, it didn't mean they were teaching Christianity.

> I looked back at the previous 10 years and realized I had spent 10 years trying to convince kids to behave Christianly without actually teaching them Christianity. And that was a pretty serious conviction. You can say, "Hey kids, be more forgiving because the Bible says so," or, "Hey kids, be more kind because the Bible says so!" But that isn't Christianity, it's morality.[2]

We can teach all kinds of morals without ever teaching the cross, which would make us no different than any other religion or even athe-

2. Phil Vischer, "It's Not About the Dream," WORLD Magazine, September 24, 2011, 57-58.

ists. Just because a church produces nice, moral, people who are good citizens in the community and never create any scandal does not mean our job is done.

Bible Knowledge

Bible knowledge is yet another quality that is a byproduct of a faithful Christian life but is not the purpose of the Christian life. Plenty of Christian kids grow up achieving gold medals at Bible Bowl every year yet drift away from the faith once they reach adulthood. Plenty of Christian adults have been in the church for decades and know their Bible backward and forward and yet show little to no fruits of being changed by it. The habits of gossip, anger, or pride are never abated by such knowledge. Just because a church has a system for making people know the Bible does not mean the church has fulfilled its purpose.

Heaven

This may be my most controversial point, but it's one I strongly believe. The purpose of the church is not to help people get to Heaven. First of all, you would be hard pressed to find that concept stated as such in Scripture. Second, I believe the framing of Christianity as being a pass/fail between Heaven and Hell has led to many of the shortcomings we see among Christians today. The church is often hampered because many Christians have a checklist mentality, yet you can draw a direct line from that back to an over-emphasis on Heaven. If a person becomes a Christian to avoid Hell and instead go to Heaven when they die, then their Christianity will be about doing what it takes to get to Heaven. So, they're going to do whatever they feel is necessary to do so. And they won't exactly be compelled to do anything they feel is not necessary to do so. It's for this reason we hear phrases like, "The Bible doesn't say I have to go to anything more than Sunday morning worship, so I'm not going to." It's why we have self-assured Christians who think their ticket to Heaven is punched by their proper doctrine and perfect attendance.

The temptation might be to make the checklist longer, telling people that they have to attend every time the doors are open, read the Bible every day, participate in church programs, etc.—all while leaving the implication that their eternal destiny might depend on them doing so.

We already have churches full of people who want to go to Heaven. Despite that, we still struggle to get commitment out of them. We still struggle to get people to evangelize. We still are left scratching our heads when they talk about the filthy television shows they're watching or the places they're hanging out despite the sermons they've heard that tell them not to. We still have people who don't love God with all of their heart, soul, and mind (Matthew 22:16), which is the basic principle that should drive everything else we do as Christians. And, because of all of these things, we still have the 90/10 principle.

Other than the Prosperity Gospel, which is purely carnal, each of these is at least partially right. It's important to work for social justice. Without ever-developing morals and aversion to sin, one cannot be considered Christian. Knowing the Bible is critical for the Christian life. Spending eternity with God is the hope of every Christian. But none of these is the purpose of the church.

So, to continue the math analogy, now that we know all of these to be wrong answers, the only thing to do is to start the equation over. When we do so, we'll realize that it was in step number one where things went awry.

Go back to before the church was even established on Pentecost. After His resurrection and right before His ascension, Jesus left a commandment: Make disciples (Matthew 28:19). We call this the Great Commission, and some form of the Great Commission is repeated at the end of each of the four gospels and at the beginning of Acts. Before the church even existed we were given a purpose.

Read the book of Acts and you'll see that everything the early church did was dedicated to this purpose, this mission the Savior had given. They fellowshipped, they prayed, they shared, they sent, they did all of these things in support of the mission.

For the longest time, I thought the Great Commission was just about evangelism. And, truth be told, I'm not very good at evangelism, so I didn't spend a lot of time focusing on it. However, though evangelism is certainly a part of it, it's much bigger than just reaching the lost. If we reduce it to the command to evangelize and just include it as one of many things we are called to do, the equation goes wrong. Instead, the Great Commission gives the entire purpose for the church. If we follow the Great Commission, everything else falls in line.

To me, Matthew's telling of the Great Commission is the most complete in terms of our duty, so we will use it for the purpose of this chapter.

> And Jesus came and spoke to them, saying, "All authority has been given to Me in heaven and on earth. Go therefore and make disciples of all the nations, baptizing them in the name of the Father and of the Son and of the Holy Spirit, teaching them to observe all things that I have commanded you; and lo, I am with you always, even to the end of the age."
>
> Matthew 28:18-20

The structure of this section is simple, based on a command and its participles. Participles are simply terms given to explain the scope of the command. For a rough English example, let's say you tell your child, "I'm going to the store. While I'm gone, I want you to clean the kitchen, washing the dishes, wiping the counters, and sweeping the floor." The command there is "clean the kitchen." The three "-ing" words give the specifics of that command. If you return and the dishes are washed and the counters are wiped but the floor is still a mess, you would not consider the command completed. The three participles define the command.

So, in Matthew 28:19-20 we have a command and three participles. The command: Make disciples. The participles: going (given as "go" in most translations), baptizing, and teaching.

Going

You've probably heard it said that this really has the implication of "As you are going," and that's true. It's about having a mission-mindedness as we are going about our lives. As you are going for some means moving far from home as a missionary, but for most of us it means seeking the lost in the workplace, in the neighborhood, in the grocery store. The command to make disciples starts with having a soul-centric view of the world.

This is difficult, and it might make us uncomfortable. But it's at the heart of everything we're considering here. If we don't have the mindset of going, we get stagnant. We get self-focused. Evangelism grows cold. When we do have that mindset, we have the outward focus that every Christian should have. The people-mindedness Jesus showed on earth and that was continued on by the apostles in Acts is what turns us from insular customers to people who have signed on to play their part in God's world-changing mission.

Baptizing

Baptism is directly tied to the heart of the Gospel. The Good news is not just that we get to go to Heaven once we die if we remain faithful. It goes much further, teaching that as Christ died, was buried, and was raised, so we too died to our old self, were buried in baptism, and have been raised to be somebody entirely new in Christ to God's glory. The Christian life is about killing off the vestiges of the old man day by day and giving ourselves to be like Jesus more and more each day, all culminating in the final promise that we will be like Him when He returns (1 John 3:2). God has always wanted a people for Himself, yet humans have continually messed it up. Jesus made it possible for us to be formed into a new kind of human to prepare us to live with God and enjoy Him for all eternity. Baptism is where this new creation begins (Romans 6:3-4).

It's important that we understand that. When we don't, people get a false sense of what the Christian life means. For many, it means that you follow a set of steps to become a Christian, then try to spend the rest of your days living well enough that you go to Heaven when you die. This leads in either of two dangerous directions.

On the one hand, it could produce self-righteousness, where a person feels certain of their salvation because they've followed the steps to become a Christian and because they are such good rule keepers. In other words, it leads to modern Pharisaism. Or, for others, it leads to a lack of assurance. It's heartbreaking how often I've heard Christians say something akin to, "I sure hope I've done enough to go to Heaven when I die." That's the point—you haven't! You never could! Jesus did on the cross what we could never do for ourselves. We put our faith in His works, not our own, and we die in the waters of baptism to become the new creation He has brought to life.

Teaching

Of the three, this is the key to restoring the biblical vision of the church. The command to make disciples is what launched the church, and this facet is where the whole command stands or falls. Unfortunately, it often falls. When we get someone baptized and think it's our job to keep them coming to church so they can learn from classes and sermons, we have failed the command to make disciples. Even taking them through a new Christian's course, while an improvement, is not disciple-making.

I've often heard it said that the churches of Christ were once the fastest growing religious movement in the world. Some have cast doubt on that claim, and there's certainly good reason to take it with a grain of salt. In any case, what we can all agree on is that we used to be a lot faster growing than we are now. Christians in congregations across the country lament how the building used to be packed and now it's mostly empty. This is not unique to us, either. Plenty of denominations share the same disconnect regarding their booming past and their shrinking present.

I believe this final cog in the Great Commission is exactly why. We were going and we were baptizing, but we weren't finishing the job of the Great Commission in our teaching. We gave sermons and Bible classes for people to take in, but we didn't disciple them until they could be sent. It's not unlike Israel's constant cycle of repentance and restoration.

In Deuteronomy 6 God laid out the plan for multigenerational success to the men of Israel: Love God, practice your faith, and diligently teach your family to do the same. So long as one generation was teaching the next to follow God, Israel would remain faithful and receive His blessings. Just having a generation of God-fearing people was not enough. They had to pass it on. The same is true with Christians today. Cultivating individual faithfulness is not enough. We must teach people to take up this mission as their own as well.

To what end, then, should we be teaching them? Not just to the end that they understand our worship practices and can defend why they go to our church rather than another. Not even to the end that they can study the Bible for themselves. We are to teach them to the end that they become Jesus followers. This is the church's purpose. This is how we stop having customers and start having a self-feeding church. We learn to become like Jesus so we can start teaching people to be like Jesus, think like Jesus, act like Jesus.

If you think about where this final participle ends, it creates a cycle. "Teaching to observe all that I have commanded you" must also include this final command to make disciples. We haven't taught people to observe all that He commanded until people are involved in observing this particular command.

You're going to hear a lot about discipleship in the coming years as it's becoming a new church buzzword. Don't be deceived—discipleship is not merely about individual commitment. Discipleship is not discipleship unless it is done in the manner of this three-step cycle Jesus created. In other words, Jesus wanted His disciples to go, baptize, and teach until their students could go, baptize, and teach and participate in the mission of the church themselves. Jesus followers develop Jesus followers who develop Jesus followers. That's where true discipleship leads us.

Paul reiterated this cycle in 2 Timothy 2:2. "And the things that you have heard from me among many witnesses, commit these to faithful men who will be able to teach others also." There he carried the cycle out to 4 generations: Paul to Timothy to faithful men to others. Timothy's job as the preacher at Ephesus was not just to preach good sermons. He was to equip others to join him in the mission of developing disciples.

If my theory is sound—that making Jesus followers is the mission of the church—you would expect to see evidence of such sprinkled throughout the New Testament. And, as a matter of fact, that's exactly what you see.

> For whom He foreknew, He also predestined to be conformed to the image of His Son, that He might be the firstborn among many brethren.
>
> Romans 8:29

God's purpose for us is to be conformed to the image of His Son. He called us to be His people so that we could be made to look like Jesus. The idea that Jesus would be the firstborn among many brethren suggests that Jesus is the prototype, a new kind of man. We used to be men like Adam; now we're to be men like Jesus. This is a far cry from the Christianity that challenges people to try to be morally good, to learn everything they can about their Bible, or get to Heaven. The bar is raised impossibly high when we measure ourselves against Jesus. This should humble us, which leads us to continually fall back on God and the power of the Spirit to do what we can't do ourselves.

> I have been crucified with Christ; it is no longer I who live, but Christ lives in me; and the life which I now live in the flesh I live by faith in the Son of God, who loved me and gave Himself for me.
>
> Galatians 2:20

Our old self died and Christ has taken over in our lives. We are now governed by Him and His desires. We slowly die to the flesh and become alive to the Spirit in Him. We have a version of Christianity today that lets people negotiate how much of their lives they will give to Him. "I died and Jesus lives within me" leaves no room for such a "choose your own adventure" Christianity, though. Either He's fully in charge of our lives or He isn't.

> My little children, for whom I labor in birth again until Christ is formed in you...
>
> Galatians 4:19

Paul gives the purpose of his ministry as forming Christ in the people under his influence. Notice Paul did not say he was trying to get them to Heaven, or make them moral people, or fill their heads with knowledge. His purpose was to see Jesus in them.

> ...Till we all come to the unity of the faith and of the knowledge of the Son of God, to a perfect man, to the measure of the stature of the fullness of Christ.
>
> Ephesians 4:13

Paul didn't view it as just his personal ministry to help people be like Christ. As we examined in the last chapter, he explained that the purpose of the church leadership God has established is to help people grow up in Christ so they can build up the body by what they all have to contribute.

> Him we preach, warning every man and teaching every man in all wisdom, that we may present every man perfect in Christ Jesus. To this end I also labor, striving according to His working which works in me mightily.
>
> Colossians 1:28-29

Once again Paul gave the purpose of His preaching, teaching, and ministry to bring people to perfection (or completion, maturity) in Jesus.

Consider what happens when we do this, when we go back to a Christianity that is truly a CHRISTianity. Just as with a math equation, when you change step one, the outcome will be totally different. That's why we've fallen short, and that's how we can get back on track. **The biggest reason why church isn't more is that church is about something other than Jesus.**

That's the biggest problem with all of the lesser gospels. They can be almost entirely Jesusless and still function. They fall short of God's original plan for the church, and from that everything else in the equation goes wrong. Though the answer may sometimes look close, it's not the outcome God intended if we don't work the equation properly from the beginning.

Imagine the difference you'd see if a church was filled with Jesus followers rather than moral law keepers. In the same way, wouldn't it make a difference to swap out a church full of people who think it's their job to know the Bible backward and forward with a church full off people who first want to follow Jesus? Or, contrast a church full of people who are there because they want to go to Heaven with a church full of people who are striving to be more like Jesus every day. The same goes for the moralistic, or those focused first on social justice or self-esteem. Which church is going to be a brighter light to the community? Which church is going to do better at building itself up? Which church is going to glorify God more?

But, the beauty of all of this is that if we get back to the mission of following Jesus and producing Jesus followers, all those other misconceptions of the Gospel fall properly into place. A church full of Jesus followers will carry out social justice. A church full of Jesus followers will have full assurance of God's love and grace, giving them the self-worth we all need. A church full of Jesus followers will know the Bible and live moral lives. A church full of Jesus followers will most certainly have eternal life. And, oddly enough, a church full of Jesus followers will show the world a prosperity gospel the world has never seen. It won't be based in something as foolish as earthly success but rather the riches of knowing Christ and sharing His love and grace in familial community greater than any the world could ever offer.

In short, a church full of Jesus followers won't need to have their

Christianity scheduled for them by some organizational leader. They will perform the church's three-fold work of evangelism, edification, and benevolence organically, as part of who they are. Evangelism becomes something we're all working on together as people who are sent. Some will excel more than others due to their gifts, but as everyone strives to have the mind of Christ, we'll all realize that we must seek the lost just as He did. Rather than being that thing I don't talk about because I don't like to do it, evangelism becomes the thing that draws us nearer to God than ever before as we depend on Him and see Him at work.

The edification of the church no longer falls on the preacher or an elder alone. When we all are following Jesus and sharing His love, the one another commands become the duty of each of us. The older teach the younger how to be pleasing to God with their lives (Titus 2:4 comes to mind). The weak will be carried by the strong (Galatians 6:1). Jesus-like Christians will understand that they are their brother's keeper.

And, benevolence will be a way of life, much more akin to the Acts 2 model where we are taking care of each other from within and looking to distribute the good things God has given us for the benefit of our brethren. Our God is generous in all He does. To emulate Him leads us to be the same way. I'm sure you've met those people who model Christ in their benevolence, always willing to share anything when their family has a need. Imagine if every Christian were trained to view money and possessions that way. Once Christ-following takes root, the work of the church will be a daily, ongoing activity carried on by everybody rather than something subbed out to one or two talented people at the top to have them do our work for us. We start to become that holy priesthood God designed us to be.

The one problem with all of this, of course, is that it's not easy. The idea of a church that transcends what we've known and becomes like the Biblical picture is one that is easy to be excited about, but there's no shortcut that will make it happen. It will take time. It will take work. It will take dedication to a Great Commission-centric mindset of the church. A decision will have to be made if we're willing to clear the decks and start over by reevaluating everything we do and know as church through the lens of pointing people to Christlikeness.

Ultimately, we must ask which church is going to look like that which the Bible promised us, that something more. It will be the one that follows God's equation, the one made up of Jesus followers. That's why the Great Commission must be at the center of everything. It gets us back to our purpose, and once we get that right the rest of the equation falls into place. When we get that wrong, we get a weakened, watered down version of church based on man's wisdom and business strategies.

From the conversations I've had, I believe there are many who are already on that path. I believe there are many more who are on their way toward it. However, I believe there will also be many who are comfortable with things just the way they are. And, there will be those who like the idea of a church that is more but aren't willing to have the patience and put in the dedication to get there.

But what if we just took a chance on it? What if we went all in on going back to God's plan for discipleship being the driving purpose of the church? What if we truly put our eyes on Jesus and made Him the center of everything?

I believe three things would happen. I believe our familial closeness would grow to something truly not of this world. I believe our flagging evangelistic efforts would be emboldened. And I believe we would all see God powerfully at work in ways we rarely see now. I'll explain what I mean in the following five chapters.

DISCUSSION QUESTIONS

1. Which of the off-target gospels has effected you the most?

2. What are some of the differences you would expect to see in a church full of people who want to be like Jesus compared with a church full of people who want to go to heaven?

3. How can you participate in the Great Commission cycle in your life?

5

TOGETHER

The most important sign of an authentic discipleship is
Jesus-like love. It is not a worship experience. It is not experiences of the Holy Spirit. It is not correct doctrine. It
is not faith. It is not service to the needy... Jesus-like love
is both the environment and the fruit that God wants to
see produced in his church.

Bobby Harrington and Josh Patrick[1]

IN THIS CHAPTER AND the next we'll examine what it means to
live like Jesus in the context of our church family. Before we get started,
though, I want to remind you of the disclaimer offered in the introduction: I'm painting with a broad brush by necessity. This is the topic about
which I receive the most pushback, as many are quick to tell me how
loving their congregation is is. Keep in mind that because of the broad
brush, not all of the criticisms offered and changes suggested will apply

---

1. Bobby Harrington and Josh Patrick, *The Disciple-Maker's Handbook*, ePub
Edition, Grand Rapids: Zondervan, 2016. 65.

to every congregation. These chapters might not apply to you at all.

On the other hand, I ask that you keep an open mind. Like the Thessalonians you may be showing great love, but perhaps the call to "excel still more" is needed. I know the kind of New Testament love and community about which I'm writing does exist, but I'm also of the opinion that it's exceedingly rare and most of us have never experienced its full power. I believe that with God's help it's possible, and that's what I want to see come to pass in every congregation.

What would it look like if Jesus were a church member like you and me? That's the question each of us has to ask ourselves. If we're going to be like Jesus in all things, that clearly includes our involvement with the local church. What would His weekly involvement with the church be? How would He connect with His church family? In a broader sense, we should also ask what it would look like if a church was filled with Jesus lookalikes and people striving to be Jesus lookalikes. How would they go about their lives? How would their actions and structure differ from ours? Would that church have providers and consumers? Would that church have set meeting times and scheduled programs, then let everybody go about their lives the other 164 hours of the week? Would each of those Jesus lookalikes check "church" off a list every week and move on? Would they consider their lives their own?

If discipleship means following in Jesus' footsteps and becoming like Him, then one of the surest signs of successful discipleship would be outward action. Jesus did not come to earth and merely exemplify a private, devout walk with the Father. Instead, His life was spent denying Himself to give to others, love others, serve others, teach others, and ultimately save others.

And yet, for many the term discipleship means having a strong personal walk with God. Because we live in an individualistic society and because Western culture is based heavily on the rights of the individual, we tend to read the Bible from an individualistic mindset, too. Maturity means battling sin well, having a good prayer life, and following a good pattern of study. Taking up your cross and denying self means having a consistent personal commitment to God. Countless books written on the Christian walk—even useful ones written by faithful, grounded men and women—focus on this "you and God" dynamic.

The consumer/producer dynamic of "churchianity" just furthers this problem as the implied message is that *we* are here to help *you* grow and get to Heaven. Many of our sermons are on how *you* can walk more closely with God. *We* offer age- and interest-specific classes to help *you* improve in some way.

We sometimes use terms like "serving the church" to refer to a brother helping with building upkeep, or leading a prayer in the worship service, or running the audio system, or to refer to a sister decorating for VBS or changing out a bulletin board. These are perfectly fine and good actions, but what we mean when we ask people to commit and serve the church says a lot about our understanding of the church. These things further the "individual contributing to an organization" mindset. "Serving the church" should mean serving the people of the church in some way.

In like sense, we've probably all heard the phrase "We don't go to church, we *are* the church." In my experience, the phrase has been used to communicate ideas like the need to be committed to church attendance or carry out the Christian's call to live differently than the world. To the early Christians, though, being the church also meant thinking about and living for their family.

To borrow an analogy from the sports world, consider the differences between baseball and football. Of all the team sports, baseball puts the most emphasis on individual performance. It's one pitcher at a time against one hitter at a time. Football, on the other hand, arguably puts more emphasis on team performance than any other sport. Every play involves every player on the field for both teams working toward their team's goal. We tend to treat church like it's baseball—we all do some things together, but in our daily lives we're standing at the plate on our own, relying on God to not strike out by sinning and hoping to do some good while we're at it. The New Testament picture is much more like football—we're not all given the same job, but we're all working together to move the mission forward.

The entire New Testament is saturated with the idea that the Christian life is meant to be lived together rather than as individuals. Through Jesus we understand the kingdom and its "already but not yet" dynamic, where we're already living in the kingdom but awaiting the final fulfillment of it in eternity. He spent some of the last hours of His life teaching and demonstrating this to His apostles in John 13–17, where He washed their feet to teach them to serve each other, told them to love one another as He loved, and prayed that they would stay united. He said that His followers' love for one another would be our sign to the world that we are His (John 13:34-35), and our unity would be what convinces the world that He came from the Father (John 17:20-23). With that in mind, and with Jesus' teachings on the kind of people we ought to be, the idea is that we should already be living out the kind of love we will share in eternity.

Let that point sink in; the perfect, Christlike love we'll all show each other in eternity is something we start manifesting here on earth, imperfect though it may be. We are to set about loving and serving as Jesus did among one another so that, despite our limitations, we will show people what a church full of Jesus imitators looks like. And that doesn't look like everyone keeping to themselves to live privately devout lives.

Consider what we see in Acts 2. The first thing God did after saving people was to add them to the church. That's not a coincidence. Right after the thousands were baptized, the church immediately started behaving like a family. They worshiped together, prayed together, learned together, ate together, shared together, and gathered in each other's homes together. There was no sense of "go live your Christian life this week and come back on Sunday for the next lesson." The apostles and those around them understood the church as a family rather than a location, event, or organization. Their behavior matched this belief.

Further, as we read through Paul's writings we see how often his doctrinal sections break down God's plan for bringing together people of all backgrounds in one family through Christ. Then, notice how great a percentage of his application sections focus on how we should get along, care for each other, and push each other forward in the Christian walk. His epistles are positively packed with "one another" commandments (which we'll examine in the next chapter).

Over and over again we see God's plan for saving a people rather than individuals. His plan was not just about *me*, it's about *us*. For that reason, if our discipleship does not regularly lead us into the lives of those around us to love, serve, teach, and encourage, it's incomplete. It's not in keeping with God's intention for us in the New Testament. Unfortunately, the business view of church has greatly damaged this idea. We can say week after week that we're a family, but our actions will speak the truth and we will reap what we sow.

It starts with the reason why people pick a church. As discussed earlier, businesslike churches often rely on marketing principles in reaching out to potential members and evangelizing. The implied messages are "You'll enjoy our worship and sermons," "Here are the programs we have specifically tailored to you" and "Here's how we can help you get to Heaven when you die." With that as their introduction, people already understand their relationship to the church through an individualistic lens. From there it's an uphill battle to get them to think in a familial sense, and we do little to gain ground by the way we teach them.

Just looking at the setup of almost all church auditoriums alone you can tell that the emphasis is not "one another." Rather, we all come as a crowd of individuals to receive our feeding, take it home, and do with it what we will. On average, the majority will not see each other outside of the building doors during the week. I can't help but think the early church would be stunned by such a setup.

Despite this, we still know that we're supposed to have a church family for a reason. We know that there are commandments regarding what we do for each other and how we treat each other. But rather than emphasizing the familial commitments each member has and teaching them to proactively carry them out, we often take shortcuts to say those commandments have been fulfilled. Because the church's emphasis is on helping each individual in their personal walk with God and on drawing them to the building rather than sending them as little Christs, the "one anothers" just become incidental boxes to check. In other words, the Bible says we should fellowship with each other, so we have a quarterly pot luck. The Bible says confess your sins to each other, so we offer you the chance to tell the entire congregation about it at the invitation (if you've sinned badly or publicly enough, of course). The Bible says we should correct and restore one another, so we'll preach a sermon on an issue (modesty, giving, attendance, and the like) if it becomes a problem. The Bible says to bear one another's burdens, so we'll have the preacher keep office hours in case you're struggling with anything. The Bible says to serve one another, so we'll have a couple of scheduled events to give you the opportunity to do that.

When functioning organizationally like this, the church is like a community center where they put on things you can come and get involved with if you feel so inclined. Going back to the start, though, our aim must be to produce Jesus followers and then set them about the work of acting like Jesus. Do we trust them to start doing that on their own? How can they understand their need to do so in a setup that implicitly tells them the opposite?

As discipleship undergoes a revival, the worst thing we can do with it is to fold people right back into programs where they are consumers. Helping them be like Jesus includes teaching them to think in terms of community and then act on it. Just like a child outgrows the need for their parents to schedule everything they're supposed to do and stay on top of them with reminders, Jesus-following Christians must outgrow the need for the entirety of their church life to be scheduled and coordinated by the church's organizers.

For years, books have been written and articles and news segments have been done on the problem of extended adolescence. Many young people are living at their parents' home into their late twenties, often not bothering to pursue a career, get married, or even obtain a driver's license. If parents continue to pay for everything and expect nothing of their children when they grow into fully capable adults, they're actively harming them. If they can't be sent out with the expectation that they can take care of themselves and be a productive member of society, the parents have failed them.

In the same way, when a person has been a Christian for decades and their involvement in the church is little more than showing up to the building for worship and scheduled events, can we really say the equipping of Ephesians 4:11-16 is being accomplished? In other words, members should grow to carry out their Christian duty to their family organically, naturally occurring without needing their spiritual parents to schedule everything for them. Small groups, fellowship meals, and the like are all fine activities for churches to put on, but if we're not careful we can let those turn community into another box to check. But community isn't an event. It's a mindset where all of us seek opportunities to support and love each other. If we church leaders aren't training them to that end but rather making the entirety of their church life revolve around the calendar we develop, we're failing them and perpetuating the business mindset rather than the family mindset.

If as a member your commitment to the church revolves around the building and the event calendar and includes no service, hospitality, encouragement, or teaching of your own volition, I urge you to shift to a familial understanding of the church. Until we get back to that, and while church remains a collection of individuals trying to get to heaven, we'll never see a church that is more. We will continue to be the band of loosely connected individuals who have our separate lives and cross paths only in the context of the church organization.

Stretch this thinking out to its logical end and you reach the conclusion that thousands have espoused: "I don't need the church, I can come to God in my own way." That statement is obviously dead wrong and completely counter to everything we read in Scripture. Most Christians roundly reject such thinking. However, when we make church about the individual rather than giving yourself up to be part of a family, it's only natural that individuals will find they can do all of the spiritual things on their own and don't need anybody else's involvement.

For all of these reasons, we have to abandon individualism and consumerism and dedicate ourselves to rediscovering community in the way the early church practiced it. We should be in each other's lives. We should be in each other's homes. We should know about each other's struggles. We should be sharing the Word and praying together—and none of these things should be building- or calendar-dependent. We are the church.

THE BLESSING OF COMMUNITY

Why has God always focused on community? Going all the way back to His dealings with our spiritual ancestors such as Abraham and Moses, He was always talking about having a people for His own possession, a nation set apart from the rest. 1 Peter 2:9 shows us that part of God's plan with all the collective terminology used there: a generation, a priesthood, a nation, a race. The eschatological promise of Revelation 21:3 is that God will dwell with us and we shall be His people. While He loves each of us individually, His plan for us has always been seen collectively. Why is that?

We could open up a theological discussion of God's nature, since God is love, and the Trinity, since the Three in One enjoy perfect fellowship, and all of the implications that those points have for us. However, as important as those points are, that's another book to be written by someone far more knowledgeable than me. For the purposes of our study, I want to focus on the benefits we receive from living like a family. We are far better off when we sacrifice of ourselves, our homes, our wealth, and our calendars to connect with each other.

Why? Because…

Community Facilitates Love

We will dig deeper into Jesus' command to love one another in the next chapter, but before we get there it's important to realize that we can't really meet His requirement if we aren't involved in each other's lives. This is not a generic command that means "be nice to people and care for them." He meant what He said. We are to love in a way that sacrifices self for the good of others. Opportunities to share such love don't just happen, though. They come when we make a conscious effort at building relationships with those other people.

We're all aware that we live in incredibly lonely times. We think we're connected to so many people because of social media, but deep down we know that's not real. Many of us hardly speak to our neighbors. Front porches are disappearing as our homes become fortresses more and more all the time. Face-to-face conversation with anyone is hard to come by, even when we're sitting across the table from each other. Thus, a church family who is committed to being around each other through thick and thin is revolutionary in this individualistic, closed-off world. Add to this the crisis of mental health, with so many suffering from depression, anxiety, and other challenges. I'm not saying that the love of a church family will fix everything. However, having people who love you and are there for you no matter what, who know your struggles and pray for you and encourage you with the Word… that certainly can't hurt. We have something beautiful to offer in a time of such great loneliness and pain. And, last but not least, we are begging to be truly known. We have learned to create socially acceptable representations of ourselves. My social media profiles aren't me; they're an image of me I've curated for the outside world to see. The version of me that most people see and interact with is the social me. Very few people know the real me, warts and all.

This presentation of ourselves is the source of the dreaded church foyer small talk mentioned previously—"How are you?" "Good! You?" "Good!" I have no idea how many people have told me they're doing just fine when they're not, but I know it's more than a few. I've done the same thing, too. You probably have, as well. However, being in each other's lives as family makes it impossible for me to look perfect all the time. And when we let people see our shortcomings, and they love us through it, it does two things for us that we desperately need: it keeps us humble, and it makes us feel a deep love and appreciation for them.

None of this is possible so long as we stick to a version of church that keeps us from truly connecting with others. When church life means regular, organic interaction, though, the opportunities to love abound.

Community Facilitates Holiness

We know God wants us to be holy, set apart from the world (1 Peter 1:15-16). However, we also know it isn't easy. Spend just a little bit of time trying to be perfectly sinless and close to God, and you'll see just how impossible it is for us to do so. So, in His perfect wisdom, God surrounded us with other imperfect people who are on the same journey. He gave us people who have been where we are and can show us the way. He gave us people who are right where we are so we can help each other stay strong. And, He gave us people who are fighting battles we've overcome so we can turn and help them. Holiness works much better as a team effort than as an individual pursuit.

For just one example, consider the statistics on pornography. A 2014 Barna Group survey found that 64% of self-identified Christian men and 15% of self-identified Christian women viewed pornography at least once a month. A 2016 Barna survey showed more hopeful numbers, but they still found 41% of practicing Christian young men between age 13-24 were viewing porn at least once a month.[2] Like most sin, porn addiction thrives on darkness. When we let it stay in the dark it quietly kills off or hampers the spiritual lives of thousands of men and women—probably even millions. They fight the addiction on their own, terrified of what people in their church family might think if they found out.

That's just one example of many. Consider more socially acceptable examples like gossip, lying, being overly critical of one's spouse, or any number of other sins. We all have struggles in all kinds of different forms. This is exactly why God has no intention of making us fight our sins alone. He instructs us to confess our sins to one another (James 5:16) and, rather than judging and shunning, He commands the strong to gently turn back the weak and the erring (Galatians 6:1-2; James 5:19-20). Giving people verses and sending them home to fight the battle alone

---

2. "Porn Stats," Covenant Eyes, covenanteyes.com, 2018. 22.

was never the plan. God gave us a family to help make us holy.

Community Facilitates Discipline

Church discipline is a difficult subject. The prospect of confrontation isn't fun for any of us, and the idea that we may have to ask somebody to not return is especially challenging. However, functioning as a family gives this uncomfortable task a whole new light.

First of all, it changes the nature of the rebuke. The closer you are to someone, the more their criticism means to you. If the rebuke comes in the form of a sermon from a preacher we only speak with in passing on Sunday, it's rather easy to miss or ignore. If it comes from an elder you barely know, it's easy to blow off. But if it comes from someone who you truly view as a loving family member, you're far more likely to listen.

Second, it maximizes the effectiveness of the rebuke. If the rebuke amounts to little more than telling the person to find a different building to spend an hour in every Sunday, not much change will come about. On the other hand, if discipline means losing a family of people who care for you, check in on you, and make you feel loved, the impetus to change is so much stronger. God's plan for discipline was predicated on making the sinner not just choose between the far off, more abstract concepts of Heaven and Hell, but the real life, in-the-now choice of the pleasure of sin vs. the love of a family. When faced with the prospect of losing something irreplaceable, we're far more likely to respond to discipline. When we behave as a family rather than a business, God's design for discipline becomes so much more powerful.

Community Facilitates Equipping and Growth

There's a reason Jesus picked a select few to train for three years rather than simply preaching sermons to the masses over and over. Sermons and Bible classes have to be one size fits all, but disciple-making requires personalization. A sermon has to be preached to people of all levels of spiritual maturity and Biblical knowledge. Relational teaching is able to meet people where they are and answer their questions, correct them when needed, and challenge them to grow at their own level and pace.

There are all kinds of quotes from great men of the faith telling us how important the pulpit is and how the church's well-being depends on what is said from the pulpit. In my experience, though, the kitchen table is just as valuable, if not more so. If your Christian life felt stagnant and you felt insufficient in your knowledge, which would help you more: one or two sermons or Bible classes, or an hour across the table from a couple of mature Christians who would be able to answer your questions and teach you what you need to know?

Jesus modeled an approach we would do well to emulate. While He preached messages to the masses (like the Sermon on the Mount), with His disciples He brought them up in their understanding and responsibility as one does a child. He showed them the truth and embodied a loving, serving ministry. Then, He did those things alongside them, sending 70 out on the limited commission and teaching them and answering their questions when they returned. Finally, after His resurrection He was ready to send them out on their own. Leading, then working alongside, and finally sending. That process took three years of relational teaching, though. In those three years His apostles needed corrections, specifications, and answers to questions. The opportunity to tell Peter "get behind Me Satan" arose because He was spending time with Peter and regularly conversing with him. He set the apostles straight regarding who would be greatest in the kingdom by being around them and listening to their conversations.

Yes, Jesus' ministry was public in many ways, but His most enduring work of training others was done through close relationships with a small group of followers. Most (if not all) of the strong Christians I know can point to a faithful disciple or two who took the time to build a relationship with them and teach them the faith. Sermons and Bible classes have value, and we should continue to make use of them. But we must realize that in order to reach the final goal of bringing someone to maturity in Christ, it's going to take more than one size fits all lessons. It's going to take family relationships.

Community Facilitates Evangelism

We'll get into evangelism more in a later chapter, but for now we'll let it suffice to say that Jesus had high expectations for the community of believers as an effective tool for evangelism. In John 13:34-35 He said that by loving one another as He loved us we'll show the world we're His, and in John 17:20-23 He said that the unity of His followers would be what makes the world believe that He came from the Father. That's the difference between inviting people to our church and hoping they like it and inviting people into a family of loving believers who are sacrificing for each other's sake week in and week out.

Community Facilitates a Greater Love of God

Finally, the closer we are with one another, the more we'll all love God and be thankful to Him for the great design He had for the church. We begin to see people as God sees them, which helps us realize how God views us. We'll see the value He has placed on us when we place that kind of value on others. God's command of self-sacrifice can be difficult. It hurts. It takes our entire lives to learn it, however imperfectly. The more we do it, though, the more we are called to remember that we're only trying to imitate what He did for us.

And, we'll see the great patience God has toward us. When we're committed to loving one another, tolerating one another, and being patient with one another, we get a glimpse of God we can't get anywhere else. Because it can be incredibly difficult to bear with a brother or sister who tests our patience, it's in those moments that we see a fraction of how patient God is toward us. When Christianity is the individualized "you and God" pursuit we've come to know, there's little requirement for this. We just sit on the other side of the building, or move to the congregation down the road if things get bad enough. But when we commit to our family with Biblical love we learn the difficult lesson of being long-suffering and we see just how amazing it is that God loves us despite all we do to hurt Him.

RECENTLY MY WIFE AND I have started working on puzzles at night after our daughter goes to sleep. It's a great way to put our phones down and talk to each other while doing a hobby together. The problem with puzzles, of course, is that it's fairly common for pieces to go missing. Unsurprisingly, it's even more common when you have a toddler who can reach the edge of the table.

One lone piece might seem small, but it means a lot when you're trying to complete the puzzle. The pieces around it are noticeably incomplete without it. On the other hand, when that piece goes off on its own, it is fairly useless. It was designed to fit in with the rest of the puzzle and be a part in something much bigger than itself. The puzzle needs the piece, and the piece needs the puzzle.

So it is with the individual Christian. As long as we as church leaders cater to a group of individuals and make them dependent on us rather than on each other, our puzzle will remain full of holes. Likewise, so long as members consider themselves unattached and live their Christianity out as individuals, we'll simply be a box full of disconnected pieces. The sooner we start to think of ourselves as a small part in something bigger than ourselves, the sooner we start to build the beautiful, Biblical picture of the church God gave us.

DISCUSSION QUESTIONS

1. What is the difference between a "me and God" view of Christianity and a Christlike view?

2. What is a practical way you can connect more with your church family outside of church-organized events?

3. What are some of the other blessings that can be fully realized only in the context of close-knit, familial community?

6

ONE ANOTHER

Just as garden plants thrive in the texture of abundant sunlight and rainwater, the texture in which discipleship thrives is family.

Mike Breen[1]

AS MUCH AS IT PAINS me to admit it, I've never been a good basketball player. My organized basketball career consists of one summer church league in which I put up somewhere in the range of seven points, a handful of assists, and maybe—*maybe*—ten rebounds. That wasn't my per game average. That's total. For the whole season. Sure, I had plenty of chances to take open shots, but I almost always deferred because I had no confidence I could make them.

If I wanted, to, though, I could make it my passion to get good at basketball. I could spend two or three hours on the court every day, dribbling up and down the floor and shooting hundreds of jump shots and

1. Mike Breen, *Building a Discipling Culture*, Third Edition, 3DM Publishing 2009. Kindle Edition. 7.

free throws. I'm not saying I'd ever be great at it, but that would undoubtedly improve me as a player. However, if I did that for months, just me, the ball, and the hoop, I'd be in for a rude awakening the next time I got back in a 5-on-5 game. Sure, I'd be much improved, but adding teammates and defenders changes everything. You have to learn to work with your teammates—to pass, to set screens, to provide spacing. And, having opponents who are trying to stop you from taking good shots and are also putting you on the defensive is a wildly different proposition than taking jump shots and layups in an empty gym. The point of basketball is not to be really good at shooting in an empty gym. It's about teaming up with four other people to defeat five opponents.

In the same sense, Christianity is not just about getting good at observing religion on our own. As we saw in the last chapter, the Christian life is about giving ourselves up for God's purposes in the context of a family. Paul's body analogy passages demonstrate the gifts and strengths God has given you were given to bless others (Romans 12, 1 Corinthians 12, Ephesians 4). For the weaknesses you have, He's blessed you with a family who can build you up and strengthen you (Galatians 6:1-2, Hebrews 3:12-13). We were made to need each other.

While the first step is to start thinking in terms of community, family, or a team rather than seeing ourselves as individuals, the second step is to see what the Bible tells us to do in that community. The New Testament is packed with "one another" passages, outlining just what life in that community should look like. Unfortunately, the "one another" is often seen as a generic reference to the people around us. In New Testament terms, it's specifically about the family God has created. The picture painted is one of a group of people controlled by the love of Christ to care for others and be cared for by them. When He commands you to love others as better than yourself, it's because He's commanding them to do the same in return. It's a picture of people putting their time, their money, their preferences, and even their well-preserved self-image on the line because God has surrounded us with people who will do the same for us. It's a picture that looks like what the early church did in

Acts.

You might already be working to dismiss this concept. It seems unrealistic. It seems like a great way to get hurt (and honestly, it is). It seems like something with which it would be difficult to get other people on board, even if I did commit to doing it.

However, as Jesus followers, none of those things are our concern. Our concern is simple: What would Jesus do? He laid down His life for His friends. He got hurt in the process in ways we can't even fathom. But, discipleship says, "Where He leads, I'll follow." And, while our minds might become concerned with the end result, keep in mind that Jesus' sacrifice was more than worth it in the end, for His sake and for ours. We're entrusting ourselves to the God who never lets our efforts for Him go to waste. And, that's why He gave us one another.

In this chapter we'll look at the New Testament's "one another" commands in order to reexamine the picture of the church the New Testament gives us. The term itself implies a mutual sharing, the opposite of a consumer-provider setup. To use the restaurant illustration again, there is no counter dividing those who do the work and those who benefit from it when the phrase "one another" is in use. These are things we do for our church family and they do for us, because we're all striving to be like Jesus and these are the things He would do.

Love one another.

We'll start right at the top with the command that is the lynchpin of the church's life together. You might be tempted to skim over this as we're all familiar with the "love God, love others" call that most congregations echo. However, it's important that we take a minute to focus on what Jesus really said to the disciples and how it differed from other discussions of love.

Previously He ranked "Love your neighbor as yourself" as the second greatest commandment (Matthew 22:39) and in the Good Samaritan parable He explained to us how our neighbor can be anyone and everyone (Luke 10:25-37). It's a call to take the inward care and concern we have for ourselves and apply it to others. Stop and think about it for a minute and you'll realize how difficult it is to apply this day in and day out.

However, as Christians we're called to an even higher standard. Jesus didn't just tell His followers to love one another. He didn't even say "love each other as you love yourselves." No, He took it to a whole new level. "A new commandment I give to you, that you love one another; as I have loved you, that you also love one another" (John 13:34, repeated in 15:12).

"...as I have loved you..."

I'm not sure we've really processed how difficult an assignment He gave us with this commandment. This commandment came right on the heels of Jesus washing His disciples' feet and directly before He was to head to the cross. Again, He's not just calling us to love each other as ourselves. Instead, He's calling us to love each other better than ourselves, to deny ourselves in favor of caring for and serving our fellow Christians. He's calling us to lay down our lives for each other (15:13).

Most Christians are familiar with John 13:35. In fact, we often sing about it—"They'll know we are Christians by our love." That verse only makes sense when paired with the commandment in the prior verse. We aren't going to stand out if we love each other the way the world loves. We're going to stand out if we love as He loved.

Peter helps us understand this point in 1 Peter 1:22: "Since you have purified your souls in obeying the truth through the Spirit in sincere love of the brethren, love one another fervently with a pure heart." Once our obedient purification leads to a sincere love of the brethren, we're commanded to excel into a fervent love for each other. In this verse we see the two common words for love in the Greek, *phileo* and *agape*. Peter is saying, "You have *phileo*, that brotherly love for each other. Now convert that into *agape*, a self-sacrificing love." In practice, businesslike church assumes *phileo* as a necessity, but *agape* is optional. If you'll remember, this very distinction between the two loves carried a deep meaning for Peter. In John 21:15-17 he had that famous exchange with Jesus where

Jesus asked if Peter *agape* loved Him and Peter would only say he *phileo* loved the Savior. When Peter called his readers to grow from brotherly *phileo* love for each other into *agape* love, he of all people knew exactly what he was saying. We need brotherly love for each other, but we can't stop there. It has to grow into something more, something weightier.

Why? Because we are to be disciples of Jesus. Philippians 2:5-8 tells us exactly what that means. The very Creator of the universe forfeited His rights for us, came to earth and lived as a man for us, humbled Himself to be a servant for us, and died on a cross for us. That's the level of love to which we're aspiring. After all, that section begins with the command to "Let this mind be in you which was also in Christ Jesus..."

Consider each other better than yourselves.

In telling us to "Let this mind be in you," Paul was drawing on Jesus' example in Philippians 2:5 because of what he had told the Philippian Christians to do in 2:3—put off selfishness and pride and "in lowliness of mind let each esteem others better than himself." This is the demand of Christlike love. Again, it's not just "love your neighbor as yourself" but "love your neighbor better than yourself." He wrote similar thoughts in Romans 12:10: "Be kindly affectionate to one another with brotherly love, in honor giving preference to one another." The increasingly popular idea that a person can be a Christian without a church family and "come to God in their own way" is completely incompatible with this concept. In the same way, the idea that we can be nice to each other on Sundays and then go about living our separate lives won't fit here either. When Jesus called us to deny ourselves it wasn't just for our personal relationship with Him. It was also so He could use us as His servants in relation to others.

The infamous (perhaps apocryphal) story about the church splitting because they couldn't come to an agreement over the color of the carpet would certainly be in the purview of this commandment. How can people who view others as more important than themselves be so adamant about getting their own way that they'll break unity over something so petty? It's simple. Businesslike church does not ask us to view others as more important than ourselves. A person's affiliation with such a church literally starts with the church asking "What can we do for you?

I've heard from preacher friends who share the frustration of the rampant consumerism in Christianity today. We all see it, and we've all dealt with it. We have to realize our responsibility in creating it, though. Sure, consumeristic Christians will be held accountable for their own attitudes and actions. But we in leadership have to bear some of that accountability, too. We cannot be surprised when the people we bring in as consumers end up acting like consumers. If we consistently send the message that the person's attendance and giving matters so greatly to us, it should be no surprise when they hold that attendance and giving over our heads to get their own way and have no interest in self-sacrifice.

When we teach people to act like Jesus, though, the principle of putting others over ourselves—our comfort, our preferences, our idiosyncrasies—begins right at the top.

Confess your sins to one another.

This is a big one. It's one of the biggest factors standing between the way man does things and the way God would have us do things. It's vitally important that we enjoy each other's company and get along, but plenty of social clubs can boast that same kind of unity. Biblical, Spirit-driven unity is not based on superficial characteristics, but on our weaknesses and our common dependence on God. You might love your church family, and you might be close with your church family. But who knows your struggles? Whose struggles are you helping carry?

Logic tells us that confession was not intended to be an event or something we do only when we've committed a "big" sin. If we're all commanded to confess our sins to each other (James 5:16) and we all sin regularly, then confession should be a regular feature of the Christian life. In our business model of church, though, we've created a convenient invitation at the end of the sermon as our shortcut to carrying out this commandment. You might need to confess something, so we're providing you a time, a place, and a person to listen to you. As usual, though, when we take shortcuts we end up with a cheap knockoff of what God told us to do. We end up with a format that most Christians will never use. And, since this is the picture of confession in many Christians' understanding, if they don't do it at that time they don't do it at any time. Why not? Because confession means telling dozens (if not hundreds) of people—mostly strangers—about our struggles. Because confession means being an inconvenience by making the scheduled church time run long. Because, while having our church family pray for us helps, we know that if we tell everybody, that makes it the responsibility of nobody to follow up and keep us accountable.

We tell people that God has given us everything we need to overcome sins, and yet so many still struggle in silence. What we forget is that one of the greatest tools God gave us in the fight against sin is a family of people who love us, who are on the same path as us, who can encourage us day after day (Hebrews 3:13) and who can set us straight (James 5:19-20). As long as confession is relegated to the invitation, though, confession will remain relegated to an event. On the other hand, when we've developed the kind of spiritual relationships a church family was meant to have, then we can open ourselves up to this beautiful gift God has given us.

Such talk of confession and accountability will make some nervous, and that's understandable. Movements in our recent history have taken this concept too far, placing unbiblical burdens on people and keeping people locked up under fear and paranoia. For that reason, it's important to clarify what I don't mean and what I do mean.

This doesn't mean telling somebody every single time you sin or keeping a logbook of sins to hand over. It doesn't mean having a lone, authoritative person to whom you report, giving them untoward leverage over your life. Instead, it means building natural relationships with fellow Jesus followers who can offer us a safe place to open up about our sins. It means having teammates, spiritual siblings whom we can trust and can offer a place of trust in return. This gives us the ability to talk about those day-in, day-out sins that often get ignored or left to silent struggles—"I've been really hard on my spouse and kids lately." "I just can't seem to stop struggling with lust." "Gossip is a big challenge in my life." "I've really drifted from God. I'm not studying and praying like I should."

Some people have the opportunity to have those conversations. Many do not. The "one another" element of this commandment envisions a church in which we all have the kind of relationships where we can share our struggles with trusted brethren. If we are not pursuing a culture where confession is something each Christian practices (and not just on extreme occasions), we're settling for a shortcut and denying ourselves the blessings that comes from sharing our struggles and receiving the help God gave us.

Three blessings in particular stand out. Confession is one of the best ways to defeat sin, getting it out of the darkness and exposing it to the prayer, wisdom, and accountability of our brethren. Additionally, confession brings us closer to God by keeping us humble. At all times we're either trying to prove our own goodness or relying on God's goodness. Through confession, we regularly remind ourselves of God's goodness to us. Last, confession naturally also brings us closer to one another. It builds our relationships on who we really are rather than the perfectly preserved images we like to present. As Dietrich Bonhoeffer wrote in his classic work *Life Together*,

> It may be that Christians, notwithstanding corporate worship, common prayer, and all their fellowship in service, may still be left to their loneliness. The final breakthrough to fellowship does not occur, because though they have fellowship with one another as believers and as devout people, they do not have fellowship as the undevout, as sinners. [2]

2. Dietrich Bonhoeffer, *Life Together*, San Francisco: HarperOne, 2009 1st Edition. 110.

It's very difficult to stand over a person with pride when he pours his heart out to you and you do the same to him, sharing the ugly parts of our lives that we might prefer to keep hidden. That kind of closeness—to be known at our worst and still loved—is what we're all longing for. We can only get that by confession.

Bear one another's burdens.

On the other side of the equation from confession is the call to bear one another's burdens (Galatians 6:1-2). This command (and its parallel in Romans 15:1) is given to those who are spiritual. So, in order to bear others' burdens, we first have to grow toward that image of Christ. Once we do that, we'll start to love them enough to make ourselves available to them and listen to them. That means clearing time for them on our schedule. That means putting our phones down. That also means learning to listen without interrupting, interjecting with our own stories, and making it about ourselves. It sounds like a simple enough command on paper, but the self-sacrifice involved requires a great deal of practice and commitment.

I'm the type who is more than happy to bear another person's burdens and never tell anybody about my own, which is prideful and disobedient to God. Others are humble enough to open up their lives to others but never listen in return, which is also disobedient. There's a beauty in reciprocation, though. God gave us people we can help, and He gave us people who can help us. Humble, loving self-sacrifice leads us to practice both.

In the businesslike church, though, there's little need for this. The customer has little motivation to care about other customers. As Cain asked, "Am I my brother's keeper?" In the Biblical view of the church, it should hurt each of us when people abandon our Lord or stumble in their faith. To use the New Testament metaphor of the church as a body, when a man or a woman deserts the church, it should feel like an amputation to the rest of us. That pain must get the attention of all of us and affect our actions.

"But that's the preacher's job" or "that's what the elders are there for" are the views held—whether implicitly or explicitly—by many. As a preacher, few things make me happier than when I find that a member beat me to make a call or a visit. When the preacher calls the person who has been absent, in my experience many take it as a professional rebuke rather than a brotherly plea. When I make a visit, some see it as me just doing my job. But when "one another" reach out to help bear a burden, it sends an entirely different message. It's a sibling reaching out in love.

This is one of the great blessings of the New Testament church. You are weak, but God has given you family to help you in your weakness. They are weak, but God has given them you to help them through their struggles, too. You are strengthened by their strength; they are strengthened by yours. What we have no hope to do alone, we accomplish together.

Tolerate, bear with, and forgive one another.

Lest anyone get the wrong idea that such a church would be a utopia where everyone is always on the same page and never has any conflict, we find verse after verse telling us what to do when—not if—we clash (Mark 9:50; Ephesians 4:2, 32; Colossians 3:13; James 4:11). Though we strive to follow Jesus, we still won't fully remove our selfish tendencies overnight. This isn't a flaw in the design, though. It's a natural side effect of the fall.

We humble ourselves before one another, give preference to one another, and put others as more important than ourselves because that's what Jesus did for us. Consumeristic Christians, on the other hand, have no motivation to work through differences. Since they come to church for what it offers them, if they don't like something about the experience they don't have to put up with it. They can simply sit on the other side of the building from the people they don't like or go to another church if they can't work out their conflicts. Some of them just stay home and cite all of the hypocrites as the reason they don't have any interest in the church. I don't say this to downplay the pain that some have experienced from bad church situations. There are plenty of cases of real abuse or mistreatment that went unacknowledged and unchanged. However, to say everyone who leaves a church over conflict had such a strong reason would be incorrect. In light of the commandments to bear with, tolerate, and forgive one another, giving up and moving on (to another congregation, not to stay at home) must only be a last resort.

Without this command, all the rest flat on their face. It's an integral piece of God's structure because if we don't have to work through the tough times together, our love for one another will only be as deep as each person prefers it to be. We'll never trust one another enough to confess our sins and lean on each other. And, we'll always have the implication that we have the final say on the relationship since we get to pull the plug whenever we want. That's incompatible with the commands to humble ourselves before one another and serve one another.

"Be hospitable to one another." "Pray for one another." "Consider one another." The list could go on and on, and some will be covered in later chapters. The point I hope I've communicated in the last two chapters is this: God intended our Christianity to be a shared experience rather than an individual pursuit, and in the one another commands He outlined what that experience is to look like. A family full of little Christs will go about their lives loving and prioritizing each other in this way. A building full of customers will not.

To illustrate this idea, consider two cars starting in two different locations and setting out to two different destinations. As their journey begins, their paths may very well cross or even be shared for a while. In the end, though, they will still end up in those different destinations.

In the same way, businesslike churches may show love, may facilitate confession, and may see people bear one another's burdens and tolerate one another in love. The longer the journey goes on, though, the more divergent the roads become. One starts by bringing people in according to what they want in a church and makes the final destination each of their personal salvation. The other starts with a self-denying relationship with Christ based on the Great Commission and makes its final destination a Christ-emulating, God-glorifying, mission-bearing family. It's only natural that the depth of the one will produce different results than the other in the long run.

As the two roads diverge all the more, all of our practices in what we consider "church" will take on a new light. Some differences will be more notable than others, though. Among those evangelism may be the greatest, as we'll examine in the next chapter.

DISCUSSION QUESTIONS

1.   If Jesus were with us physically today, how would He carry out the one another commands in the context of the church family?

2.   What is the practical difference between "Love one another," "Love your neighbor as yourself," and "Love one another as I have loved you"?

3.   Do you have people to whom you can and do confess your sins? Do you have people who confess their sins to you? If not, why not? If so, how have those relationships benefitted you?

7

"GO" VS. "BRING THEM IN"

Every Christian here is either a missionary or an impostor. Recollect that. You either try to spread abroad the kingdom of Christ, or else you do not love him at all. It cannot be that there is a high appreciation of Jesus and a totally silent tongue about him.

Charles Spurgeon[1]

AS THE O'JAYS SANG in 1975, "You got to give the people... give the people what they want."[2] Such has become the philosophy of churches in the attractional era. The accepted proposition is that a bigger church means a more successful church, so the key is to find ways to get more people in the door. The more a church employs this philosophy, the more businesslike they become. And the more businesslike they become, the

1. Charles Spurgeon, "A Sermon and a Reminiscence," The Spurgeon Archive, archive.spurgeon.org/s_and_t/srmn1873.php, April 3, 2020.
2. The O'Jays, "Give the People What They Want," Survival, Philadelphia International, 2008. CD.

more their attempts at growth look like that which comes out of a marketing textbook rather than the Scriptures.

As discussed in chapter 2, the business model of church is dependent on this marketing in much the same way a restaurant is. The organization's success is dependent on its ability to offer a product people want and then advertise that product in a way that draws the people in. The product varies by congregation, from lively worship, to dynamic preaching, to programs directly targeted at various demographics (youth, singles, seniors, young families, etc.), to whatever else a congregation views as its selling point. The advertising method also varies, although the methods are typically the same as are available to any organization—location, signage, mailers, online/social media presence, and perhaps television or radio commercials.

Since the church is dependent on what it can offer to bring people in, evangelism often consists of telling people how much they'll love your church and why it's the church for them. In trying to attract people, there are a few options available.

Entertaining Worship

When I was a kid, my family changed congregations as our former congregation began to get more and more "innovative" in worship. When my parents met with the elders to ask why or what the Scriptural basis for such decisions might be, an elder explained that they had to "push the envelope to get more people in the door." In other words, their plan to increase attendance was to keep finding ways to "spice up" worship. A few years later we saw some friends who still attended there and got the chance to ask how things were going. Their teenage daughter revealingly replied, "Well, it's not as boring as it used to be!"

In a culture that values personal feelings over everything else, it's no wonder that many are seeking a kind of spiritual high from worship. If that's what people want, then you can be sure there will be those who are ready and willing to give it to them. Once that happens, the temptation is to make the work of the church all the more focused on the Sunday production. Some churches have even begun calling the Sunday meeting their "Worship Experience," telling people right up front that the worship is about them and the feeling they take from it.

Faithful churches know that cheapening God by trying to entertain people is not an acceptable way to evangelize. Still, it's possible to rely on worship as our draw even without ever resorting to entertainment. The experts tell us what to offer, how long the sermon should be, how many songs to sing, and when the worship should be wrapped up, all so we can know what people are seeking and make sure to offer it for them. The idea taught is that before we give consideration to God as to what would please Him and what we have in our hearts to pour out before Him, we must first place boundaries on it so we don't spend too much time doing so. The visitor is the focus of the worship. Others emphasize the importance of good, energetic singing as the element that will impress people about the church. However, some congregations just weren't blessed with an immensely talented song leader. Some churches are made up of older people who have to sing a little more slowly and softly. In all honesty, in some congregations the worship, while heartfelt and passionate, just isn't going to be the kind of thing that wows the person who wanders in off the street. That is only a death sentence for the church if we assume our ability to attract people is our only way to grow and perpetuate the church. We want to offer good worship to God, yes. But if we're relying on our worship as the key to bringing in outsiders, we're operating on an unbiblical foundation.

We still want our worship to be passionate and energetic, sure, but if we walk away having pleased the masses without considering God's desires, the point has been missed. We gather together to "offer the sacrifice of praise to God, that is, the fruit of our lips, giving thanks to His name" (Hebrews 13:15). Worship is about coming together to "with one mind and one mouth glorify the God and Father of our Lord Jesus Christ" (Romans 15:6). We gather together to worship Him, not ourselves, and not our visitors. Marketing our lively worship experience is not the same as evangelism.

Programs

People need a place to connect right when they walk in the door, so you'd better have something for them. If they have teenagers, they're going to want a youth group. If they have young kids, they're going to need a Bible class program, an annual VBS, a camp, and possibly children's church. If they're unmarried, they're going to want a singles/young professionals program. Because that's what people want in a church, and we've got to give the people what they want. The church—a family in name only at this point—couldn't be more segmented. But that's alright. The numbers look good, and that's what counts, right?

And, the truth is, some congregations are simply too small to offer the kind of programs that consumeristic Christians are seeking. Neither the people nor the resources are available to them. If the marketing experts of today's Christianity are to be believed, those churches' chances are slim. Small churches frequently see families drive past them to the bigger churches every single week because they can't offer programs. I've had people echo this sentiment to me at both of the congregations with which I've been blessed to work. They say things like, "If you guys get some more young people you can really grow." What if we don't? Where is the Scripture that says, "And the church grew because they had kids and so other people with kids wanted to join them"? Only an unbiblical, businesslike model would consider a church doomed if they are unable to offer programs. This is not evangelism. It's marketing.

Dynamic Preaching

So much of today's understanding of the church is targeted at the importance of the pulpit. Selecting a preacher is not unlike a sports team's process in hiring a coach. Those in charge of the decision know that the next guy could be the difference between improvement and serious regression.

What kind of system would God have designed if He needed world class lecturers to make the church grow? How can someone read the New Testament and come away with the idea that evangelism is reliant on a talented few who make for intriguing listening on Sunday? He didn't design such a system, and one cannot find that idea in the New Testament. It comes from a marketing-based ideology that sees our Sunday showing as our opportunity to reach people.

The numbers alone tell us that there aren't enough highly talented speakers to go around. There are thousands of churches and yet transcendent speakers are few and far between. If we're dependent on the preacher's oratory skill to bring people in, many congregations are going to struggle. That's not a shot at any of the faithful, hard-working men filling pulpits. It's simply a fact that being a high-level public speaker is a skill reserved to a small percentage of the population. Speaking as objectively as I can, I'm a decent preacher. I do my best to always faithfully speak truth, and I've been told I communicate ideas clearly. But nobody would call me dynamic. I am not a great orator. If my congregation's growth was based on how engaging and polished my sermons are, we'd probably be in trouble. "We have a great preacher, you should come hear him" is not evangelism, though. And thank goodness it isn't.

Truth

We had the big idea. Everybody recalled the great success of the tent meetings of days gone by, and so we were going to bring it back. We rented a local event center. We printed up advertising cards to hand out all over town. We chose a simple, non-threatening topic: "What Jesus Can Do for Your Life. We ran an ad on local TV programming. We posted flyers in the local diners. And, in a town of roughly 5,000 people, our congregations combined to distribute 2,500 cards. Some of us went old school and even knocked some doors. Our people were talking about the event to folks everywhere. As the event came around, I couldn't have been prouder of the efforts made by the Christians in our area. And on the night of the big event, we opened the doors to a crowd in the range of 120 people—no small feat in such a small area.

There was only one problem: There was not a single person in the building who was not a member of one of our participating congregations. After all of that effort, not a single lost, non-Christian soul attended the event. In the aftermath a few discouraged Christians offered the reason they had decided on for why the plan didn't work: people just don't want to hear about Jesus anymore. Our culture's moral decline means people have no interest in listening to the Bible, they concluded.

While it's understandable why some would come to that conclusion, two problems cast doubt upon it. First, the first century church's rapid growth did not occur in a safe, God-friendly environment. They brought countless people to Christ despite preaching to idolatrous, wildly immoral cultures, often while facing heavy persecution. Second, the idea that people don't want the Gospel anymore was directly controverted in our own county. One of the brothers involved in putting the event together had led 11 people to the Lord that year. How did he do it? He talked to them about Jesus and asked if they wanted to study about Him. That's it. People were still interested in the Gospel. They just weren't interested in giving up their night to walk into a building full of strangers to hear what they saw as our interpretation of the Bible. Honestly…who could blame them?

In the days after our failed attempt I started noticing a number of ads for other religious events in the area. Some even put up billboards and sent out mailers. And each time I saw one of those, I didn't give it two seconds of thought. That's when the realization hit me—if I'm not going to go to their events, to be in a room almost entirely filled with strangers, to hear somebody I don't know talk about something I might not even believe, then why would I expect them to come to ours?

This is often the last resort though. When a church won't compromise worship, can't offer targeted programs, and doesn't have a world class speaker in the pulpit, we comfort ourselves by saying we have the truth. And we tell people they should come to us because we have the truth. When they don't, some deduce that the lost just aren't interested. We got spoiled by the days of the tent meeting, when we could put up a tent, set out a sign, and have people come piling in to hear the Bible. That's just not our world anymore, but that doesn't mean the Gospel has no place in our society.

While this may be the closest to true evangelism of all the methods mentioned, it's still reliant on marketing. Now that it doesn't work that way, we can either conclude that there is no hope to reach people or conclude that setting out the Word and expecting them to come to us is no longer a viable system.

Where Marketing Takes Us

The plan is to get them in the door and make sure they like it while they're there. Evangelism, then, consists in having members invite their friends based on what we can offer them. But is that winning people to Christ? Or, rather, to our church's offerings? Is that the message the early church preached? Mark's Gospel shows us that many were only going to be interested in Jesus for His power to heal, and for that reason He repeatedly instructed those He healed to refrain from telling anyone. In John 6 He drove away those who only wanted Him for His ability to feed them. In Jesus' estimation, the motivation that brings a person to Him matters.

For that reason, we should give strong consideration to how we aim to reach people. We should note that only one of the practices mentioned above (entertainment as worship) is objectively wrong. We should also note that much of these efforts come from a good heart. So if these methods are not wrong, why are they a problem? Why shouldn't we use such marketing tactics?

In an earlier chapter I used the analogy of separate pathways. When you have the choice of going one direction or another, each step down one path leads you even further from the other. When we start in a place other than self-sacrificial devotion to Christ and following in His footsteps, each subsequent step in our growth will look increasingly different from the plan God had in mind. Two major shifts come to mind as a natural result of this choice.

A DIFFERENT METHOD: "GO" VS. "GET THEM TO COME TO US"

Jesus did not tell His disciples to find a good location, find out what the people want, and get them to come to you. He told them to go. He didn't tell them to be magnets, drawing people in. He told them to be salt and light. Going is part of an attempt to make disciples, while getting them to come to us creates customers.

It's an undeniable, biblical truth that we reap what we sow. If we sow a message that reaches out to customers, we're going to get customers. And, as the old saying goes, what you win them with is what you win them to. If you win them to any of these things that have been offered to attract them, they'll keep coming as customers to be served. However, as we studied previously, our job is to help them become conformed to the image of Christ, servants committed to doing God's will. But customers aren't servants. It's exceedingly difficult to flip someone's mindset from being a consumer who's in it for what they get out of it into a servant who's in it for God and for the people around them. To do so is to pull a bait and switch on them, and nobody likes a bait and switch. The person who comes to a restaurant to pay for a meal does not bus tables or fill drinks. There is no self-sacrifice in being a customer. For this reason, we do people no favors when we feed into their consumeristic tendencies. The consumer looks for a church with a mindset that says "Church is about me." A church that markets to such consumers tells them "Yes it is, and here's what we can offer you."

A DIFFERENT MESSAGE: "JESUS IS LORD" VS. "YOU'D LIKE MY CHURCH"

The other shift from New Testament practice to businesslike practice involves the message itself. At its root, evangelism is about telling people the good news. Jesus laid it out for us in Luke 24:46-48: "Then He said to them, 'Thus it is written, and thus it was necessary for the Christ to suffer and to rise from the dead the third day, and that repentance and remission of sins should be preached in His name to all nations, beginning at Jerusalem. And you are witnesses of these things.'" The Bible tells us elsewhere that the good news is the death, burial, and resurrection of Jesus (1 Corinthians 15:3-4) and the arrival of the kingdom (Matthew 4:23). The message the New Testament church took to the world was just that simple, and we would be foolish to try to outsmart it or dress it up.

Yes, there's much more that can and should be said regarding the Gospel, and the New Testament fleshes that out. But the two basic points Jesus offered at the end of Luke do a great job of capturing what the lost need to know, namely that the Savior went to the cross and came back from the dead (establishing His lordship), and everyone should repent, turning from their own way to submit to His.

As Luke's Gospel flowed into his account of the early church given in Acts, this is precisely the message we see them preaching: Jesus is the Lord raised from the dead, so all must repent. It was Peter's message to the Pentecost crowd in Acts 2, highlighting the resurrection (2:29-32) and calling them to repent and be baptized (2:38). It's what Peter also preached to the crowd who gathered in Acts 3, once again calling on the resurrection as evidence (3:14-15) and urging repentance (3:18-21). And, it's what Peter told the council in Acts 5:30-31. Though Paul had to preach the message from a whole different angle to a Gentile crowd on Mars Hill in Acts 17, the crux of His message was the same—God calls you to repent because there is One who will return to judge you, and you can know this is true because the One was raised from the dead.

When you read through Acts, notice what they didn't do. At no point did they put out lures to bring people in and then try to teach them the Gospel. They didn't see themselves as an organization with a number of offerings. "Jesus is Lord; repent and follow Him" and "Come to my church; you'll really enjoy it" are not the same message. "You'll really enjoy it" isn't the good news, and if it's not the good news then it's not evangelism.

The main point: Jesus is the message. There are different ways to present Jesus as the message outside of just preaching—particularly our example of what a group of Christ followers looks like—but the message has to stay centered on Him.

A FAMILY WITH A MISSION

Because of these two shifts, we should expect a different look and different results. Consider the path of one who has been won to Jesus-following rather than to a congregation and its offerings. From that starting point, the road toward maturity and bearing fruit is so much clearer.

First of all, we realize our job is not done with them at baptism, nor after they have completed a new Christians study. It is not done when we have them attending regularly. Our job is not done until they have grown and matured to the point of being a producer, exercising their gifts for the good of those around them and exemplifying Christ. It's the Great Commission cycle of Matthew 28:19 at work. And, since they don't begin as a customer, it's just that much easier to help them transition from target of the mission to participant in the mission.

So, as we help them grow in the faith, we also help them see that they are a part of the church's vital mission to reach the lost with the Good News. We teach them that by our words, but we also teach them that by being a Great Commission-practicing church who are constantly emphasizing growth and service and regularly praying for the lost and thinking of ways to reach the world for Christ. In this process, we help them learn what they need to know to participate in the spreading of the Gospel. There are plenty of Christians who know they are supposed to evangelize and even want to but fail to do so because they don't feel they have the knowledge necessary. Through personal discipleship we help them gain that knowledge and give them the confidence to sow the seed and let God worry about how the seed is received.

One crucial key to this approach to evangelism is the team spirit involved. If we are a community of Jesus followers who are regularly involved in each other's lives, it provides a radical shift from the feeling that we're sent out on our own to try to succeed. We are not left to do this alone. Instead, we pray together. We share names of people to lift them up together and pray that the Word would reach them through us. We pray for boldness. We pray for opportunity and eyes to see it. As we share these prayers, the motivation to keep trying grows as there's both encouragement and accountability that comes from working together.

Then, we have access to the two greatest tools for evangelism that we've been given: love and unity. As we looked at before, Jesus calls us to self-sacrificial love. The church is to be a group of people who are denying themselves to put each other first. That's a beautiful, rare sight, which is why Jesus said that kind of love would be how people know we are His disciples (John 13:35). Later in that same section, Jesus said our unity would be what shows people that He really was sent by the Father (John 17:20-23).

I recognize that apologetics have their place. It's important that we be able to answer the hard questions people might have. However, I think we can rely on logic and argumentation too much sometimes. Jesus told us our greatest apologetic would be our unity. The early church displayed this beautifully, as young, old, male, female, Jew, Gentile, slave, master and people of all other kinds of cultural demographics came together on equal footing. Just as it's important that we ourselves think of the church as a family rather than an organization, we also need to work to help the world see us as a family of people who follow Jesus rather than the organization they know it as today. They need to see the true nature of God's kingdom as the direct opposite of the kingdoms of this world. It's different. It shows people we're living for something else. If Jesus expected unity to be what shows people He is real, who are we to think we can come up with a better method?

This unity and love are what we looked at in the previous chapter. It's not just that we get along and like each other. It's not just that we have fun times together. It's that we're living for a kingdom that's not of this world, and we've all committed to abandon ourselves in service of that kingdom. If in our evangelism we can introduce people to that, and they can see from the outside that our lives are dedicated to something different than the things everybody else lives for—money, pleasure, comfort, security—our message suddenly has that much more weight. Just as the Savior intended.

Another benefit of evangelism in a familial church setting is that everyone's gifts begin to have a chance to shine. God made us all different, and He's blessed us all with different ways to contribute to the church. Some people are just going to be better evangelists than others. And honestly, I'm not very good at it. I know I'm supposed to evangelize, so I pray about it and I keep making my efforts. Here and there I break through with some folks. But the fact of the matter is, there are people in my congregation who are just better at speaking to people and sharing Christ with outsiders. In a businesslike church, their gift might never come to the surface. They might not ever be given the push to develop in that area. But in a family, as we all aim toward reaching the lost and start equipping people toward that end, the people God has gifted for that service will emerge. God has a part for every person to play. It's important that we create an environment in which each one has a chance to step up in service of the mission rather than the church organization.

Finally, one of the other great benefits that comes from a church that organically spends time together and builds each other up is this: We get in the habit of talking about the Bible with other people. I find that even with fellow Christians it's sometimes hard to turn conversations toward the Scriptures. It's just easier to talk about the weather, the latest sporting events, or how our week went than to bring up what God's doing in our lives or what we're learning in our personal study. But, as Tim Chester and Steve Timmis observe in Everyday Church, "If you find it hard to talk about Jesus with Christians, then how do you expect to talk about [H]im with unbelievers?" Once we get in that habit, it's just that much easier to strike up those conversations with the lost. The more time I spend in conversation about the Scriptures, the easier it is to turn conversations to the spiritual. The more we share the Word with each other, the easier it is to bring up a question or share a thought.

SPINNING PLATES

A family of people trying to follow Jesus and point people to Him is just going to look different from an organization that is trying to attract people. We think we have to parse out different functions of the church like evangelism, worship, edification, and benevolence and approach them all separately. For this reason we often have to prioritize and choose which functions will receive our attention and resources. We're trying to keep a group of people happy, engaged, and well-attending internally, and if we're struggling with that, it's easy to let the other things slip through the cracks. It's difficult to keep all the plates spinning, and sometimes one or two of them hits the ground.

But the Great Commission cycle doesn't separate these things. It understands that the church exists for mission. Going and baptizing are part of the plan, after which we teach them to observe all Christ commanded, leading to a worshipful, benevolent, self-feeding body of believers who understand the importance of evangelism. The church doesn't need a church growth program. The church is a church growth program.

A church will either be dedicated to attracting and keeping consumers or to reaching and developing co-laborers for the mission. There is no middle ground. The choice is ours, whether as members or as leaders, as to how we're going to pursue this goal. Start with mission. Start with Jesus. Start with the message of Lordship, resurrection, and repentance, and let everything else fall into place.

DISCUSSION QUESTIONS

1. What was the New Testament church's message to the lost? What are some of the messages most commonly used to reach the lost today?

2. Do you find evangelism difficult? What part of it challenges you, and how might more frequent spiritual connection with your church family help?

3. Why did Jesus put so much emphasis on our relationships with each other as an evangelistic tool?

8

OUT OF GAS

Stop helping God across the road like a little old lady.

U2[1]

IMAGINE, FOR A MINUTE, your car runs out of gas and comes to a stop on the side of the road. The car isn't going anywhere on its own, clearly, so your passenger gets out to push. The car begins its slow crawl toward the gas station at a few miles per hour. After a couple minutes, somebody sees your predicament and joins in to help push. It isn't much, but at least you're moving a little faster. Another mile down the road a couple of more bystanders join in. Now the car is rolling along at a pretty good, steady speed, for being manpowered. Another mile down the road, someone gets a bright idea. It's a windy day. You have a thick blanket in the trunk. What if a makeshift sail was put up? So, with 4 pushers and a sail, the car rolls right along. It's getting up over 15 miles an hour!

---

1. U2, "Stand Up Comedy," *No Line on the Horizon*, Universal - Island Records, 2009. CD.

After a few minutes you see a gas station coming up on the right. Obviously, you need gas. But this project has been a lot of fun, and after all, you're moving way faster than you ever thought possible. Sure, the pushers are probably going to get burnt out soon, the great innovation of the sail probably isn't adding anything, and the whole operation looks ridiculous compared to what the car was originally designed for, but you're proud of this project. It's really turning some heads.

What do you do? Stop for gas…or keep rolling?

The architects of modern churchianity would just keep on rolling. And they have for decades, pushing a goofy-looking manpowered contraption while ignoring the chance to fuel up and get the car running as it should.

To complete the analogy, the fuel upon which the church runs is God. He meets us in prayer as we strive to meet Him. He gives us His Word to teach us. He pours out His Spirit to mold, strengthen, and equip us. We need Him more than we can ever put into words. It would be utter foolishness to try to move our lives and the church forward without Him fueling everything we do.

At some level we understand these points. We sing hymns like "I Need Thee Every Hour." The sufficiency of Scripture has been a core doctrine for centuries. But do we believe these things as it pertains to the church? Do we need Him every hour in the work of the church? We believe in the sufficiency of Scripture for church doctrine, yes. Do we believe the Scriptures are also sufficient for church practice? If not, why not? When our plans for growth are handed down by the latest mega-church-produced book about how to market the church and how to use your building to let the community know your church is active, are we relying on Him every hour? When we're depending on the newest research on what millennials are looking for in a church and what kind of activities are likely to interest Gen Zers to determine what our Sundays will look like, how dependent on Him do we need to be? Are we adding sails to try to give speed to our gasless car?

Let's say all the church marketing strategy books, blog posts, and podcast episodes vanished overnight and we were only left with the Bible to reach people in our community. Let's say that we can't afford a building, a website, or any kind of advertising. Would we still have a hope of effectively evangelizing? The brand-new church we see in Acts did. Can you imagine handing the Antioch church a book that details how long the sermons need to be to keep visitors interested, or explaining to the Jerusalem church that they needed proper signage or people would never be able to find them? As with the car, we have to ask ourselves, what was this thing supposed to look like and how does it run?

As always, I offer the disclaimer that I'm not calling these aids and ideas sinful. However, as I've written repeatedly, the road you choose in the beginning goes a long way in determining where you end up. Therefore, the question must be asked—are we making our plans from the latest trends and then praying God will make them work, or are we starting with prayer and the Scriptures and acting on them instead? Do our actions say that we are so dependent on God's help that we would have no hope to succeed without Him? Jesus, painting Himself as the vine from which all fruit originates, told us that "apart from Me you can do nothing" (John 15:5b). We would do well to believe Him.

Man attempting to give God a hand with His plans is nothing new, though. Biblically, we can go all the way back to Genesis 16. There Abraham and Sarah (then known as Abram and Sarai) decided that if Abraham was going to have that son that God had promised, it would probably require another woman. "So Sarai said to Abram, 'See now, the LORD has restrained me from bearing children. Please, go in to my maid; perhaps I shall obtain children by her.' And Abram heeded the voice of Sarai" (Genesis 16:2).

Of course, we know how that turned out. All kinds of strife and conflict ensued (16:4-6; 21:8-21), and God had to inform Abraham that no, Ishmael was not the son who had been promised (17:18-21). Their attempt to help God fulfill His promise was a disaster. Not all such attempts will turn out so poorly, of course, but it's a direct reminder that if God promises something, He's strong enough to make sure it happens.

For all of these reasons, we should concern ourselves deeply as to whether we're operating in God's strength or on our own wisdom, talents, and resources. We are a movement that has a power unlike anything the world has ever seen. The worst thing we can do is to get in our own way by over-emphasizing our own wisdom.

There are three areas in which we can either depend on God or depend on ourselves: Bible study, prayer, and the Holy Spirit.

BIBLE STUDY

I assume it's fair to say anyone who has picked up this book and stuck with it thus far is in agreement that the church must operate according to the Bible rather than man's wishes. The Word of God is given for equipping the man of God for every good work, so if we in leadership are going to do our job of equipping we had better be helping them grow in the Word.

What can't be misunderstood, however, is our purpose for studying the Bible. Not all Bible study is created equal. Growing up, I had pages worth of Scriptures memorized. I participated in Bible bowls. I did every bit of Bible class homework I was ever assigned. I had a daily Bible reading streak that lasted years. I say all of that not to pat myself on the back, but to share it as a cautionary tale. All that knowledge didn't draw me closer to God or change my behavior. It was just knowledge, no different than the sports statistics I had memorized. I know my story isn't unique—there are plenty of adults who have Bible bowl medals from their youth in a box in the attic who could tell you that it had little effect on their lives. There are people with terabytes of Bible trivia stored in their minds who exhibit no fruit of the Spirit whatsoever. In helping each other learn the Scriptures, there must be a purpose behind our efforts. Knowledge for the sake of knowledge was not God's intention.

On the other hand, just because we have a purpose it doesn't mean it's the right purpose. One of the biggest ways we make this mistake is to study with the purpose of being right. The Pharisees had plenty of knowledge, too, but the purpose behind their study was to establish a legal code they could use to look down on others. It's important to use the Bible to establish doctrines for salvation, worship, and the like, but constantly hammering the doctrinal differences we have with others is a misuse of the Scriptures. Scripture was given, 2 Timothy 3:16-17 tells us, so we can do exactly the kinds of things discussed thus far: teaching, reproof, correction, and training in righteousness. The purpose is to bring us to a place where we are equipped to do the good works God expects from us. In other words, they are given to make us Christlike.

Instead of pursuing that purpose, many today use the Bible in the same way the Pharisees did, establishing a list of external doctrines and judging themselves on that rather than washing the inside of the cup (Matthew 23:25-28). If you can quote every single verse on baptism and craft the case for why you worship the way you do but the Scriptures aren't having a daily transformative effect on your life, you're missing the point. In Hebrews 5:12-6:3, the writer chastises his readers for getting stuck on doctrinal milk and not moving on to maturity in which they have been trained to discern good and evil. That doctrinal milk ("repentance from dead works and of faith toward God, of the doctrine of baptisms, of laying on of hands, of resurrection of the dead, and of eternal judgment") is exactly what many Christians get stuck on today and never move past. Baptism is important. The judgment is important. Nobody is saying that those things shouldn't be taught. But that needs to be course 101 in the journey of following Jesus rather than the summary of one's education.

Jesus-following discipleship must teach people to handle the Word rightly (2 Timothy 2:15), bury it in their hearts through memorization (Psalm 119:11), and meditate on it regularly (Psalm 1:2). As James taught, we are to use it as the mirror that shows us what needs to change in our lives (James 1:21-25). Every Christian must grow to a place where the Bible is challenging, pushing, and transforming them. That's the true power of the Word. Anybody can memorize verses and trivia. Anybody can come up with a list of dos and don'ts. God wants to write the word on our hearts first, though.

In a time where Biblical illiteracy is widespread, it's imperative we get back to being people of the Book. We're no longer living in an era in which everybody or even most went to Sunday School their entire lives. Some do need to be taught the basics, all the way down to the books of the Bible. Like the Ethiopian eunuch of Acts 8, they need someone to explain to them what they're reading. And that's okay—they just have to be expected to move beyond that limited knowledge in time. What matters is that we have an expectation that people grow in their knowledge of God and their ability to share Him with others. Any time there is a Christian who has been part of our family for years and can't explain anything about the Scriptures beyond the plan of salvation, or who can't profitably study it for themselves, it must be looked at as a failure. We must realize that as long as we're comfortable with Bible illiteracy among the membership, we're allowing the church's effectiveness to be hindered. The church's measure of God-given strength is directly proportionate to how much we're instilling the Scriptures in each other's hearts and minds.

PRAYER

Why would we need prayer if we've already made our own plans for growing the church? That's not to say that businesslike churches don't pray. But there's a large difference between asking God to help us with what we've already planned to do rather than putting our plans at His feet and asking for guidance. To draw on Abraham's example, when we do the former, we're asking God to bless Ishmael rather than accepting that He might have another child in mind.

Prayer is all about dependency, though. In prayer we're telling God by implication that we recognize our own inability and are asking Him to intervene. We know we are dependent on Him for everything we do and realize we shouldn't expect any results unless He goes with us.

Jesus' prayer life sets a strong precedent for us. In Mark 1:35 He rose before sunrise to get away to pray. A little bit later in Mark 6:45-46 He sent the crowds away and had the disciples get into the boat so He could go pray on the mountain. In Luke 6:12 He spent the whole night in prayer before choosing His apostles. We're also given two accounts of the prayer He taught His disciples. The prayer focuses on the physical, relational, and spiritual concerns we all have and emphasizes having an eye toward God's kingdom. And, of course, we know His prayers shortly before His death. In John 17 He prayed for His disciples, with great emphasis on their unity and their need to be "in the world but not of the world," as we have come to phrase it. We have His prayers in the garden that the cup would pass from Him depicted in Matthew, Mark, and Luke's Gospels. And, we have His words directed to the Father when He, the Son, was on the cross. Luke 5:16 gives us the best summary of our Savior's prayer life: "So He Himself often withdrew into the wilderness and prayed." In short, prayer was an irreplaceable part of Jesus' life and ministry. The implication of all these passages is obvious: if God the Son felt prayer to be vitally important, we should too.

Beyond that, though, we can also take from this the point that His prayers had a clear focus on the spiritual above merely the physical. He prayed before choosing the Apostles, He taught them to pray for the kingdom to come and for God's will to be done on earth as in Heaven, and He prayed for their unity.

The first century church's example beautifully illustrates how Jesus' followers should model their prayer life after His. After Jesus' ascension, Acts 1:14 tells us His followers were coming together and devoting themselves to prayer. That word devoted is the same root used for Cornelius's personal attendants in Acts 10:7, giving the idea that these men were those who stayed by his side to attend to him. Similarly, devotion to prayer carries that idea of sticking with it, having it constantly by our side. It was something into which they were putting serious time. That devotion to prayer was mentioned twice more in Acts 2:42 and 6:4, and their actions showed that such devotion permeated the life of the church in its infancy.

In the book of Acts we see the church praying without ceasing. They prayed as they awaited the events of Pentecost (1:14). They prayed before appointing Matthias (1:24). They regularly prayed together after the 3,000 were baptized (2:42). They prayed for boldness after they were met with early persecution (4:24-30). They prayed before commissioning the deacons (6:6). Saul (Paul) prayed while awaiting Ananias (9:11). Cornelius was praying before his own conversion, as was Peter (10:2, 9). The church prayed while gathered together before Peter's release from prison (12:5, 12). They prayed before sending Paul and Barnabas out as missionaries (13:3). Those two prayed before commissioning elders (14:23). Paul and Silas prayed while in prison (16:25). Paul was praying when he was appointed to go to the Gentiles (22:17-21).

Not only were they devoted to prayer, making it a regular part of their lives, but they also were committed to pray before every move they made. So much of what happens in the book of Acts happens *after* they prayed. They knew they had work to do for the kingdom, and they knew they had no chance of doing it on their own.

I doubt any reader needs me to belabor the point that prayer is important. If you've been a Christian for any time at all you've heard plenty of lessons about the importance of prayer. However, it's a critical distinction whether we truly depend on prayer as the power of the church or if it's something we do as just another of the many things we do. But how do we know if we're relying on prayer or just using it as an add-on?

First of all, we know how we view prayer by the time we spend on it. Just look at your habits. If the church family is regularly taking time to set everything else aside and pray, it's a good sign. If you spend time in prayer before undertaking any new ministry or effort, it's a good sign. Both are what the fledgling church did because they knew there was work to do and they knew they were powerless to do it alone. I'd go so far as to say that a church has no hope of being what God intends it to be if they are making their decisions apart from prayer or aren't regularly gathering to pray.

Beyond our collective gatherings, we can also take time to personally gather with a few others to pray. Few things bless the Christian's life more than sitting across the table from a brother or sister and growing closer to one another by sharing requests and praying for each other and for God's will to be accomplished in each other's lives. One of the most powerful things I ever experienced with church family happened when a brother suggested a few of us spend some time in a shared fast with a specific request to pray about, culminating with a prayer meeting at the end of it. That's the kind of thing the early church did. It's the kind of thing that tells God we are dependent on Him and fully expect Him to act on our behalf. It's the kind of thing that makes a true difference.

And, of course, we can't always be gathered together. That's why it's so important to also take time to pray *for* each other in our personal prayer lives. If you've never segmented up your church directory and prayed through it a few names and families at a time, it's a practice I highly recommend establishing. When you do, not only are you asking God's blessings on them, but you're also training yourself to be mindful of them. It puts them in your thoughts, which helps us keep our eyes open for chances to serve them. And, you have the opportunity to have conversations with them where you can tell them you're praying for them and would like to know if there's anything specific you can add. If we truly believe we are helpless without God's hand, we'll take the time to prioritize praying both for and with our church family.

Secondly, the value we place on prayer is seen in the content of our prayers. If you got the chance to ask a favor of the President—anything you wanted—and you asked him to commission a peanut butter and jelly sandwich to be made for you, the only conclusion others would draw is that you had no idea what all was available to you. In the same way, if our prayers are only focused on the temporal, it shows clearly that we don't realize the eternal weight of the things we can ask of God. As John Piper has often written and preached, "The number one reason why prayer malfunctions in the hands of believers is that they try to turn a wartime walkie-talkie into a domestic intercom."[2]

Listen to the prayers said when the church is gathered week in and

---

2. John Piper, *Prayer: The Work of Missions*, Desiring God, https://www.desiringgod.org/messages/prayer-the-work-of-missions, April 3, 2020.

week out. Consider your own prayer list. Where does the focus lie? Those words go a long way toward showing what has been prioritized and what people have been trained (or not trained) to ask of God. When we have the proper understanding of prayer's effect on our spiritual lives and the life of the church we still ask for God to heal the sick, but we also realize that we should be just as vigilant to regularly pray for the spiritual health of our brethren. Notice Paul's prayers in places like Ephesians 1 and Ephesians 3—how his great desire for them is to know the love of God and be strengthened by Him. That's the kind of thing we pray for our brothers and sisters when we have a sense of God's mission and grasp what prayer can do to help us accomplish it. When we have the proper understanding of prayer's effect on our spiritual lives and the life of the church, we stop asking God to make a clear path for us and start asking Him to strengthen us for whatever path He has for us. That's exactly what our brethren did in Acts 4:29-30. Where we might pray for safety and an end to persecution, they prayed for boldness to speak regardless of the consequence.

Bottom line, when we have the proper understanding of prayer's effect on our spiritual lives and the life of the church, what we say is markedly different. We pray things like "Father, remove any area of comfort that is keeping me from depending on you," "Give me the opportunity to bless and encourage someone today," "Help me to see opportunities to evangelize and to be bold enough to take them," and "Show me where my life is not lined up with Christ's example." Expect change to happen when you regularly pray these things. It's a bit frightening to leave so much open for God to do with us what He wills, but that's what faith is all about. When we ask Him to remove our comforts, He will. And when we lose our comfort, it definitely hurts. In the end we know we're better off for it because it draws us closer to Him. The same goes for praying that He show us where we're falling short. It's embarrassing to have our imperfections brought to our attention, but we know we can't move forward until they are. Praying spiritual, mission-minded prayers tells God we know the risks and yet we still have every intention of moving forward because His will comes first in our lives. As the church, every Christian must be taught the habit of praying big, scary, open-ended prayers for God to use us in His work and then preparing ourselves as though we expect Him to do so.

Beyond the Word and prayer, though, we have a promise that the prophets foreshadowed for the age of the church and that Jesus promised to give to those who followed Him. The living water Jesus promised for all who come to Him (John 7:37-39) must be pursued in order for the church to reach its intended design. The Holy Spirit will be our focus in the next chapter.

DISCUSSION QUESTIONS

1. What practical difference is there in reading the Bible as a transformative text rather than as a trivia book or as a legal code?

2. What are some ways we can increase our dependence on prayer?

3. What is a challenging prayer request you might add to the list of examples given at the end of the chapter?

9

HOLY SPIRIT

God's purpose is to make us like Christ, and God's way is
to fill us with the Holy Spirit.

John Stott[1]

THE BIBLE IS POSITIVELY packed with stories that highlight our human inability to be what God wants us to be. Between Adam and Eve, the post-flood society, Israel in the wilderness, Israel in the land of Canaan before Assyria and Babylon, and Israel back in the land post-captivity, over and over we see God giving people a chance to walk with Him and do His will on earth, and over and over we see them fail. It wasn't as though nobody tried. There were plenty of heroes who made great efforts to serve God. But in the end, they all failed to produce lasting change. The downward trajectory was only ever slowed rather than reversed.

Then Jesus came on the scene and changed everything. Part of the change, though, and the part that has helped His movement continue

---

1. John Stott, *The Radical Disciple*, Downers Grove: InterVarsity Press, 2010. 37.

marching on for 2,000 years, is the promise of the Holy Spirit. This is *the* defining distinction between Christians and everybody else: We walk by the Spirit. It's the difference between pushing the car and having a full tank of gas, to draw on the last chapter's analogy. As Gordon D. Fee wrote, "The Spirit as an experienced and empowering reality was for Paul and his churches the key player in all of Christian life, from beginning to end. The Spirit covered the whole waterfront: power for life, growth, fruit, gifts, prayer, witness, and everything else."[2]

All of the aspects of the church discussed so far in this book are dependent on the Spirit. We talked about how Christlikeness is the goal of Christian living. The Holy Spirit is how we grow into Christlikeness. We talked about how unity and the one anothers are an essential part of the church's life together. The Holy Spirit is where that unity and love come from. We talked about having an evangelistic mindset. The Holy Spirit is given for just such a purpose. God blessed us with His power to carry out each and every one of these.

CHRISTLIKENESS

In chapter four I made the assertion that the biggest reason church isn't more is that church is about something other than Jesus. And, because that's the case, the Holy Spirit's role has been greatly downplayed. Why? Because attempting to be like Jesus sets a number of things in motion. When you set Jesus as your goal, you open the Scriptures and you read His example. You see His perfect pattern of truth and love, of justice and mercy, of love of God and love of man. Any time spent trying to perfectly imitate such an example sends one perfectly clear message: I can't.

That's where the Spirit comes in. If we're to be changed into the image of Christ, Paul explains how it's going to happen: "being transformed into the same image from glory to glory, just as by the Spirit of the Lord" (2 Corinthians 3:18). We are just as dependent on God for our sanctification as we are for our justification. In other words, as helpless as we are

---

2. Gordon D. Fee, *Paul, the Spirit, and the People of God*, Peabody, Hendrickson Publishers, 1993. xv.

to save ourselves, we're just as helpless to make ourselves like Christ. The Spirit was given to make that happen.

That's the important distinction between how Christianity is understood by many versus what the Bible teaches. If you think Christianity is just about becoming a good, moral person, you can comfort yourself with the knowledge that nobody's perfect, so it's just about trying hard to be your best. Just read your Bible, take what it commands you, and try to do it. But Christianity is not like other religions. God did not give us a set of rules by which we can become nice, upstanding people. God intends for you to be somebody far better than you could ever manage to be on your own.

This is what Romans 7–8 and Galatians 3 teach us:

> For what the law could not do in that it was weak through the flesh, God did by sending His own Son in the likeness of sinful flesh, on account of sin: He condemned sin in the flesh, that the righteous requirement of the law might be fulfilled in us who do not walk according to the flesh but according to the Spirit.
>
> Romans 8:3-4

> This only I want to learn from you: Did you receive the Spirit by the works of the law, or by the hearing of faith?— Are you so foolish? Having begun in the Spirit, are you now being made perfect by the flesh? Have you suffered so many things in vain—if indeed it was in vain?
>
> Galatians 3:2-4

Christians aren't better versions of who they used to be. No, Christians are people who are being changed from the inside out. They're people who no longer live, but have Christ living in them (Galatians 2:20). That's why Galatians 5:22-23 calls the characteristics listed there the fruit of the Spirit. Too many people understand that list as a checklist we're supposed to memorize and try to keep. "Ok, it says I'm supposed to be loving so

I'll try hard to be loving today." That's literally the exact opposite of what that passage is teaching. Fruit is a metaphor used to refer to results, so it's notable that they're not called the fruit of our efforts or the fruit of our obedience. Instead, the list is called the fruit of the Spirit, meaning those things listed are the results of having the Holy Spirit in our lives.

When you think of a tree bearing fruit, how did the fruit get there? Definitely not by someone stapling apples or peaches to the branches. Rather, it got there as a result of nourishment from within. That's why the fruit of the Spirit is a list of characteristics to have rather than a list of laws to keep, as some mistakenly characterize it. If we're walking by the Spirit, God works in us to produce an outcome.

All of this is why a moralizing version of Christianity focused on just being a good law-keeper is so damaging. It's not about becoming a good person, it's about becoming a new person. Beyond that, it's not just about not doing bad things but by growing into the good works God has for us. And, it's not just about changing our outward actions but having our hearts changed to love and desire those changes. We can try to be good people on our own, but we can't become new people without Christ cleansing us and the Spirit shaping us.

For the same reason, the businesslike church's Heaven-focused, "you-and-God" Christianity falls short. Over the years I've seen preachers take to social media to advise their fellow preachers to take it easy on people, to realize that life is hard and busy for people, so don't push for too much. While there certainly were problems with the old school brand of preaching that constantly made people feel like they aren't doing enough, that's not what I'm talking about. When we expect little of people, it speaks volumes of our understanding of the Holy Spirit. When we present a choose-your-own-adventure version of Christianity and allow for scores of people to fade into the background, we are implying we don't trust the Spirit to strengthen them for the work. God has always used the people nobody would expect because it is in our weakness that He is glorified. The strength of the church is God's empowerment of everyone to think, act, and speak like Christ. Until we pursue that end, we can't expect to truly see His power.

THE PRIESTHOOD OF ALL BELIEVERS

God did not give us the Spirit merely for our own personal development, though. God gave you the Spirit for the building up of the church, too. However, as long as church involvement for most people means showing up to events put on at the building that power won't be seen. God didn't give each of us His Holy Spirit to get us to and from the building on Sunday.

The Spirit was given to bring unity to the church. Ephesians 4:3 is the first verse that comes to mind — "endeavoring to keep the unity of the Spirit in the bond of peace." However, the concept is woven throughout the New Testament. 1 Corinthians 12:13 reminds us that we were all baptized into one Spirit. Ephesians 2:11-22 speaks of God's plan to bring Jews and Gentiles together, which is no small feat, through Christ's work on the cross and how we as Christians now have access to the Father together through one Spirit (2:18). In 2:19-22 Paul gives the illustration as the church being fitted together (the same term as in 4:15-16) as a temple in which God dwells through His Spirit. 1 Peter 2:4-5 shares a similar sentiment, painting each Christian as a stone that makes up this spiritual house.

In other words, the Spirit dwells in all of us because the Spirit dwells in each of us, and the Spirit dwells in each of us because the Spirit dwells in all of us. This is our family resemblance. By making us like-minded with the mind of Christ, the Spirit draws us to a commonality that produces unity, and Spirit-given fruits like peace, patience, kindness, and gentleness are what help preserve that unity.

Consumers share no unity with the producers, though. In a "customer-is-always-right" culture, people are free to move on as soon as they don't like something. In that case, unity is based on personal preferences rather than on God's presence. The businesslike model of church has robbed us of the power that is found in true unity. Keep in mind it is this unity that Jesus intended as our living proof that He came from the

Father (John 17:20-23).

The Spirit was given to equip each of us for the work of the church. Jesus' words to His disciples in John 13–16 demonstrate the importance of the Spirit to the work of the church. In John 14 He promised the Spirit as comfort so the disciples would not be orphaned when Jesus left. There He spoke about us abiding in Him and the Father, and He and the Father abiding in us by the Spirit (14:16-17). In John 15 He explained that He is the vine and His disciples are the branches. If we abide in Him, He will abide in us to produce much fruit (15:4-5). If we don't abide in Him, it will be impossible for us to bear fruit.

How does He abide in us, then? By His Spirit (1 John 3:24, 4:13). How do we know the Holy Spirit abides in us? By the fruit we produce. When atheists ask us how we can believe in a God we cannot see or hear, we tell them that we know there is a God because of the evidence of His work. We see His fingerprints everywhere (Romans 1:20). The same answer is true of the Holy Spirit's work in the Christian's life. How do we know we have the Spirit? Because His fingerprints are everywhere. We continually grow and change and do the works God has given us. We bear fruit because He abides in us. The important point here is that this is a promise for every Christian. Every single one of us is meant to stay on the vine and become a Spirit-filled fruit bearer in service to the Lord.

What would accomplish more? Which would be more powerful? A church composed of Spirit-filled people who are doing God's work and building each other up, or a church with an incredibly talented minister? Regardless of what we say in response, we give our true answer by our practices. Do we work to make each and every member a contributor or do the gatherings and church life elevate the contributions of a select few? The power of the church is not the talents of the few, but the presence of God in the many. Under a minister-driven, consumer-producer system, the growth and health of the church comes down to the talents of the people at the top.

The burgeoning lectureship culture reveals our thinking on this matter. The underlying assumption is that we need to elevate the most talented and get as many people as possible together to listen to them. Every year new lectureships, conferences, and retreats get added to the calendar. The explanation is given that the Spirit works in the preaching of the Word. That can't be denied. But nowhere are we told that such preaching is only done through the pulpit by the most talented. As discussed in chapter 3, 1 Corinthians 12 tells us quite the opposite. Thus, it only makes sense that we pursue a system in which every Christian is being equipped to do so beyond just their personal walk with God. It makes no sense to rely only on the contributions of a few fruit bearers.

The question we have to ask ourselves is, do we want to pursue a system in which the Spirit can work through everybody or continue with a status quo where the church's experience of the Spirit comes in short bursts from one person two or three times per week? If we are to maximize the Spirit's work among us, we have to equip and make use of as many Christians as possible in the various roles that involve teaching, encouraging, serving, and building each other up.

EVANGELISM

In John 16:8-11 Jesus said the Holy Spirit will convict the world of sin, righteousness, and judgment. There is no true evangelism without conviction. Romans 10:17 shows us that the journey to faith starts with hearing the Good News. John 13 and John 17 show us that Christlike love and supernatural unity are the visual demonstrations of such faith that will help people know Jesus' disciples and know that He is real. In other words, the preaching and active demonstration of the Gospel is how people are won. While I'm not here to place an extrabiblical limit on how the Spirit works, doesn't it make sense that the Spirit would work to convict people of sin according to the methods God gave us for presenting the message? God's power is put to use best with God's methods, no?

Unfortunately, it's far too easy to appeal to people's carnal sides to try to reach them as carnal people. We see the worst of this in the rock concert worship settings devised in the last few decades and in the ever-popular prosperity and self-esteem gospels where the focus of the worship is the attendee rather than God. The consumeristic "If you build it, they will come" approach to Christianity, while less blatant in its elevation of the consumer, still aims to reach people in their pride rather than in their Spirit-convicted state.

It's fairly easy to discern between that which aims at building relationships with people as equals and teaching them about Jesus versus that which aims to reach a customer and make them loyal to an organization, program, or personality. One might make the argument that we should be trying to reach souls by any means necessary, but the principle of "what you win them with is what you win them to" is undeniable. And Jesus never wanted numbers for the sake of numbers. Evangelism aimed at customers produces customers, and it's hard to change a customer into a Spirit-filled disciple. The method that looks to let the Spirit work on His terms must be given preference over any other.

LET HIM LEAD

When Israel looked to go from Sinai toward the Promised Land, Moses knew that there was no point in their trip if God did not go with them all the way. "Then he said to Him, "If Your Presence does not go with us, do not bring us up from here. For how then will it be known that Your people and I have found grace in Your sight, except You go with us? So we shall be separate, Your people and I, from all the people who are upon the face of the earth" (Exodus 33:15-16).

Moses' request must be ours. Our desire should be to become a church driven solely by the power of God, the kind of church that inspires awe in each one's heart. It's time to stop pushing the car and start fueling up.

DISCUSSION QUESTIONS

1. Why is the fruit of the Spirit called "fruit"?

2. How can we sow to the Spirit (Galatians 6:7-8)? How can we do so in our individual lives, and how can we do so together?

3. Thinking outside the box of only the Sunday assembly, how can we create ways for more Christians to contribute as part of the church family?

10

TEACHING CHRIST

Amazing as it may seem, all Jesus did to teach these men his way was to draw them close to himself. He was his own school and curriculum.

Robert E. Coleman[1]

I BELIEVE EVERYBODY wants to see a church model like what's been described thus far. The idea of the church having the kind of close-knit relationships needed in order to practice the one anothers is one that is likely exciting to many. Having a church full of people practicing evangelism is every minister and elder's dream. Seeing the power of God at work in our efforts is something we all desire. The question that remains, and the question upon which this book's usefulness depends, is this: How do we get there?

Before we do anything we have to come to the realization that a change is necessary. As the saying goes, "If you always do what you've al-

1. Robert E. Coleman, *The Master Plan of Evangelism*, Baker Publishing Group. Kindle Edition, 2010. 37-38.

ways done, you'll always get what you've always gotten." Similarly, there's the ever-popular line, "The definition of insanity is doing the same thing over and over and expecting different results." And, as always, the Bible says it best — "You reap what you sow" (Galatians 6:7, paraphrased).

Going back to the Bible means first dropping any baggage we have. If we neglect to do that, we'll end up right back at the same conclusions we held before. When you go back to the various passages we've examined on God's vision for the church, there is no concept of the businesslike church we know. The biggest mistake we could make, and one we will be tempted to make, is to try to shoehorn this kind of family-oriented, disciple-making centered structure into what we already do in our businesslike churches. We have to drop the baggage.

Why? Because trying to combine family and with the businesslike model we know simply won't work. It's like trying to install Mac software onto a Windows machine. The operating system isn't equipped to run what the software tries to do. The message doesn't fit the method. If we're going to help each other stop thinking of church as a building, an event, or an organization, we have to stop treating it as those things and start treating it like the family, body, and priesthood it was meant to be. If we want to remove the producer-consumer split and truly pursue a priesthood of all believers, we're going to have to retrace our steps all the way back to step one and restart there.

What, then, is step one?

We practice the Great Commission. It was what the church was built to do, and it's my contention that a thorough, patient application of it results in churches made up of people imitating Jesus. God is smarter than we are. It only makes sense that when we pursue the mission He gave us, we get the results He expects from us. As Ephesians 4:11-16 teaches us, each one is to be equipped to grow to the point where they too are involved in the building up of the church. We aim to be people who love Jesus, want to be like Jesus, and desperately want to show everybody what He looks like. All of us. What we should aim to see is Christians doing the work of the one anothers and evangelism organically, as a natural part of their lives, rather than as a scheduled event someone else put on for them.

Of course, we all desire to see this. Every preacher I know wants those in his congregation to be like Christ. We preach sermons on the need for evangelism and teach classes on how to practice it. We teach on loving one another. We emphasize the importance of attendance and commitment to the church. We work hard to instill Bible knowledge in people. And, those who are mature Christians long to see their fellow Christians practice Christianity alongside them. Still, by and large, there's a frustration that the results are so hit or miss. As one preacher friend put it, we huddle up on Sunday, call the play, and then go out on the field and stand still instead of running the play. Next Sunday comes, we huddle up again, and start the cycle all over.

The question then gets a bit more specific. How do we practice the Great Commission? How do we set that cycle in motion?

This is where the method and the message either reinforce one another or undermine each other. To continue doing what we've always done is to ensure that it doesn't get done. The solution to almost everything has been to get people in a room and have someone speak to them. Not only do we have sermons and classes, but we have Gospel meetings, seminars, lectureships, workshops, and retreats. For years it's been my default course of action, too. We'll add another class for those who want to go in-depth. We'll move the schedule around to try to teach those who aren't as committed. We'll have a speaker come in and address a certain topic to hopefully get people fired up.

The onus is then on each listener to do with it what they will. But a 24/7 faith can't be taught in a half an hour per week. An annual weekend seminar isn't going to bring anybody to maturity. One-size-fits-all lessons can't possibly fit everybody. Study the New Testament's teaching on what the church is supposed to be and you'll quickly come to two conclusions: First, it's going to take much more than a Sunday and Wednesday gathering where most members are passive, and second, we're going to have to think outside the four walls of the building. Ultimately, we have to do what Jesus did.

How did Jesus make disciples? For Him, disciple-making was a life-style. He gave sermons and taught crowds, but among the crowds He was received with the same kind of fickle consumerism we see today, precisely the kind of thing we're aiming to avoid. He knew the work that was going to last was that which was most personal. For that reason He chose the twelve, walking with them, teaching them the truth about Himself, answering their questions, setting an example for them, and expecting them to join Him in the work. Even among those He had an inner circle of three who became the most prominent members of the church's launch at the beginning of Acts. Jesus was the greatest preacher and teacher of all time, yet nowhere do we see Him saying, "Alright, that's your kingdom class for this week! Go act on what you heard, and I'll see you next Sabbath!" If He did not expect deep, abiding change and equipping to come solely from a lesson given to the crowds, neither should we.

When we brought our daughter home after she was born, we didn't set her down and tell her the fridge and pantry were stocked with food and to help herself any time she got hungry. We didn't set a plate on the table for her at meal times and hope she showed up to eat it. She wasn't physically mature enough. She needed milk, and she needed it to be fed directly to her. Likewise, Christians don't just come to maturity unless someone is helping nourish them.

How do we do it? In practical terms, then, practicing the Great Commission means walking people through the process of maturing as a Christian. Disciples are handmade, as some have said. If you are a mature Christian, pray that God would help you choose someone (or two or three "someones") to disciple. Tell them you want to help them grow in their walk with Christ and ask them to get together with you regularly to study and pray. Teach them what it means to live for Christ and let them know that you expect them to grow to the point of exercising their gifts to strengthen the church.

As Jesus gave the limited commission and used it to teach the 70, help them find ways to live out their Christianity and be there to walk them through the questions and challenges that arise. It's in this kind of relational format where specific questions can be answered and the disciple can be helped along at their own pace. Once the disciple begins to mature, bearing fruit and showing a Christlike people-mindedness, they must be taught to continue the cycle. The end goal is not to keep feeding them forever, but to have them turn and feed others. Keep an eye on them, be there for them, and (of course) pray for them, but launch them to do the work in their own right.

If you're a church leader, I couldn't urge you more strongly to structure your efforts around disciple making. This is going to mean starting smaller than some might like. Since it can't be done en masse, choose "faithful men" (2 Timothy 2:2) and make time to meet with them or build them up. Mature Christian women, do the same for faithful women. You can do it 1-on-1 or with three or four others. Don't make the group too big, though, or some will be hesitant to open up and participate.

If you're someone who wants to get started but don't feel ready or able to disciple someone else, that's fine. You can start by doing two things: first, pray for and be looking for a mature Christian who can take you under their wing. Ask them to meet regularly to pray and study together. Second, start imitating Jesus. Start looking for people to serve, encourage, evangelize, and love. God blesses the efforts of all who want to do His work, and the process will grow you in thinking, seeing, and acting like Christ.

What do we teach? There is plenty of discipleship curriculum available, and you might find one that suits you well. Don't overthink it too much, though. Put simply, teaching people a kingdom-focused Christlikeness comes down to helping them learn three things. They need to know how to walk with God, building a devoted life of prayer and study that lead to Spirit-driven growth. They need to know how to love their church family, serving and contributing to the building up of the body. And, they need to know how they can reach the lost through prayer, love, and truth. That's it. It's easier said (or written) than done, of course, and it will take time. But on the other hand, it's not a complicated process. As a mature Christian who follows Christ, it can be as simple as teaching people to do what you do.

I shared the story earlier in the book about sitting at a ministry conference and needing a mentor instead of a lecturer. The same is true for each member in the pews. As I sat and learned and longed to be able to ask questions and share my specific struggles, that's what the Sunday listener needs, too. We can tell them to read the Bible and pray, and we can even have classes to teach them how to do so, but they need someone to model it for them and answer their questions. We can push, prod, and beg people to evangelize, but what they really need is someone to help them feel equipped to do so. We can have someone in for a week to teach on marriage development, better parenting, or financial wisdom, and those things can help. But what Christians need more than anything is someone to walk with them and guide them through these challenges.

Anyone who has had the blessing of having a mature Christian in their life to help guide and counsel them through life's challenges knows what a blessing this can be. A speaker can give all kinds of good information, but there's no substitute for someone who knows you well and has godly advice, exhortation, and even correction. It's a beautiful human relationship, and it's the kind of relationship the church was built to produce.

The world of education teaches us the same lesson. It makes a great difference to the student to have involvement from a parent or a tutor who pushes them toward achievement and helps them along the way by explaining the concepts and takes the time to answer their questions. While they learn from the classroom and can read the textbook for themselves, it's a huge boost to their learning to have someone walk with them at their own pace. Disciples need that same kind of care.

A FULL DEPARTURE

How we go about equipping people will determine what people think it means to be a member of the church specifically and to be a Christian more generally. We're either teaching them that being a Christian means showing up and then going home to live out a private faith life, or that being a Christian means taking responsibility for emulating Christ as an interconnected part of God's family.

If we're going to go back to the start and seek to reap different results, then we have to sow different seed. Though the ideas espoused in this book might be new to some readers, other readers have probably read similar thoughts in this growing discipleship movement. I'm happy to be just one of many calling for a return to discipleship-driven, relationship-oriented churches. It's a great encouragement to me to see so many moving in that direction. Where I hope to add to the discussion is in this: I hope I've made the case for a complete departure from the business model of disciple-making.

Unfortunately, a sort of hybridization is already happening. As discipleship becomes the new buzzword, the rise of the "discipleship program" as one of many programs has begun. As we discussed, the end goal of disciple-making should be to unleash people to do the work of equipping, encouraging, serving, and loving, not return them right back to a scheduled, programmatic, checklist version of church. To go back to the restaurant analogy, it makes no sense to put the time in to teach people to cook and then go back to just inviting them to keep coming to the restaurant. Obviously we're still going to gather on Sundays, and I'm not advocating abolishing class times or special events. But what we put forth as "church life" must shift from scheduled, building-centered, event-based Christianity to life-based obedience to Christ.

For this same reason I'd advise great caution in depending on small group ministries. (By this I specifically mean the program in which the church is divided into smaller groups and assigned to various meeting places in place of Sunday night or Wednesday night gatherings). I've been asked the question as I've discussed this book with others and thought it to be a necessary inclusion in this section. It's a fairly popular practice and is the answer many have turned to in an effort to get beyond the limitations of lecture-style events.

Frankly, the small group method is exactly what it would look like if someone tried to shoehorn the Biblical need for community and disciple making into the business model. Though there are great benefits to such scaled down meetings — more personalized learning, better opportunities for relationship building — it can still easily fall into consumerism since it is an event put on by "the church" (organizationally speaking) rather than an organic action taken by the spiritually mature. And, it can lead to checklist Christianity since it's a once-weekly event. Like the traditional Sunday and Wednesday events, people can complete it, check it off a list, and move on having completed "church" for the week.

In his work on the modern school system, longtime educator John Taylor Gatto argued strongly against timed class periods marked by the ringing of the bell. His contention was that the ringing of the bell taught children by implication that learning is to occur during those periods and should be brought to a halt—regardless of progress—when the bell rang. Similarly, if "church" is a scheduled thing with a set start and end, people learn by implication that such fulfills their commitment to church. Jesus' example (followed by the Acts church) was to do such activities as a part of life rather than as a scheduled event. If community and Biblical discussion are a timed event on the church calendar, that unintended consequence becomes a factor.

Once again, we should frame everything by the original goal of equipping people to imitate Christ and build each other up. If we were starting from scratch, would that be the solution we would devise—to bring people into smaller meetings, have them participate in some discussion, and go home to live out their week? Much like the Sunday and Wednesday events, that doesn't mean we need to get rid of such groups. We just have to make sure that if we're doing them that they become a launching point for greater connection and responsibility rather than an end in themselves.

We must keep the main goal the main goal. We can't measure success by numbers in the directory, attendance on Sunday, or even participation in our functions. Success is the steady development of the people in our family to maturity that leads them into full participation in the work of building up others, reaching the lost, and glorifying Christ. Everything we do must be evaluated with that goal in mind. So many of the things discussed here are not wrong. There is nothing unbiblical about lectureships, small groups, or any of these tools. We have to understand, though, that a tradeoff will be made. If our church culture is building, event, and expert-oriented, that will set the tone for what the body thinks of as church life. Those things we do that are consumer-driven send a mixed message and hurt our ability to reach our goal. How we teach is just as important as what we teach.

When I was a kid, we must have played a dozen variations of the classic game Tag. One of my favorites, though, was the version where anyone tagged by the person who was "it" joined them in being "it." The goal was to be the last person standing, which got harder and harder as more and more people got recruited into tagging others. This is the model Jesus left us. Go tag someone else with the Great Commission until they can help you tag others. One turns into two turns into four turns into eight.

I hope you'll spend some time in thought, study, and prayer on this topic. Then, I hope you'll act on it. Point people to Jesus and show them how to follow Him, one disciple at a time.

DISCUSSION QUESTIONS

1. How did Jesus teach His disciples? How did Paul teach Timothy? What would it look like for us to follow that method?

2. How does the concept of reaping what you sow apply to our methods for making disciples?

3. What would you need to learn to start making disciples of Jesus?

11

LIVING CHRIST

As we embark upon discipleship we surrender ourselves
to Christ in union with his death—we give over our lives
to death. Thus it begins; the cross is not the terrible end
to an otherwise godfearing and happy life, but it meets us
at the beginning of our communion with Christ. When
Christ calls a man, he bids him come and die.

Dietrich Bonhoeffer[1]

IN THE PREVIOUS CHAPTER we moved from theory into practice.
In order to move away from the producer/consumer split of businesslike churches to family-minded churches, the first step is teaching people one by one how to follow Jesus. The other half of the equation is
an active modeling of Christlike living. Someone who is the product of
Great Commission discipleship is one who has been taught to observe
all that Jesus commanded. They're the kind of person who is living out

---

1. Dietrich Bonhoeffer, The Cost of Discipleship, New York: Touchstone, 1995.
First Touchstone Edition. 89.

the loving, sacrificial, kingdom-minded perspective Jesus would have us embody. They then show others how to live that way and point the way, continuing the cycle Jesus gave us. In step one we teach someone how to have a walk with God. In step two we show them the outward manifestation of that walk, all of which can be summed up in one phrase: sacrificial love.

Near the top of the list of "all that Jesus has commanded" is the command to love one another as He loved us. As discussed previously, this goes far beyond the command to love our neighbor as ourselves. We are to love our Christian brethren better than ourselves because that's what Jesus did. We are to love in such a way that abandons self and puts others first. We can take this radical, against-our-nature step because we know God has us covered. We no longer have to look out for "number one" because God is caring for us in our stead, and His love never fails.

It is this sacrificial love of others that drives family-based church and that is so often lacking in businesslike church. One of the great differences between modern Christianity and Jesus' Christianity is the lack of sacrifice. By trying to make it convenient for people, we teach them it's about them. That's a message Jesus never taught. As Dietrich Bonhoeffer wrote, "When Christ calls a man, He bids him come and die." The Christian life is about denying ourselves, taking up our crosses, and following Jesus (Luke 9:23). Jesus made it clear that He expects His disciples to trade themselves in for something bigger. Sacrifice is an indispensable part of the Christian life.

What does this mean for the Christian in the producer/consumer system, though? It might mean sacrificing sin for doing God's will, or sacrificing events on our schedule to make it to church gatherings. In the New Testament's picture of church life, though, sacrifice goes beyond just our personal walk with Christ. We're expected to sacrifice for each other and for the lost. That's what loving as Jesus loved entails. Jesus gave up Heaven and all the blessings He enjoyed there to come be a bondservant and go to the cross for us (Philippians 2:5-8). We're commanded to "have this same mind" just a couple of verses after being commanded to consider one another as more important than ourselves (2:3). Paul became all things to all men for the sake of the Gospel (1 Corinthians 9:22), showing us that souls are more important than our personal preferences and comfort.

It's not just about cold, ascetic self-denial, depriving ourselves of happiness and fun to trade our way into Heaven. Jesus gave us the parables of the hidden treasure and pearl of great price in Matthew 13:44-46 to show us that the kingdom would be worth anything we have to give up. Both paint the picture of someone being so excited by what they've found that nothing they have is too high a price to pay. What this means in practical terms is rearranging our lives around accomplishing God's will. Everything we do is something we'd be willing to trade in if it furthered the work of the kingdom. This can take a number of different forms in our lives. I'm certain I will not manage to cover them all here, but these prominent ones must be mentioned.

We must be sacrificial with our time.

When I first moved out of my parents' house and got my own place, my mom and sister were determined not to let me have the stereotypical bachelor pad. They stocked the kitchen with all kinds of cookware (much of which went unused), put a few pictures on the walls, and gave me a plant for "greenery." I did not want a plant. In my mind, I did not need a plant. I said as much. Nevertheless, when they rolled out of the driveway and left me to the house alone, I had a plant.

I was told it needed water every two weeks, but I wasn't exactly regimented in keeping that schedule. What usually happened is that I would forget to water the plant, a few weeks would pass, it would start to wilt, and once it got bad enough, I'd finally notice the plant had turned into a yellowing, dried-up shell of its former self. So I'd grab a cup of water, give it the nourishment it needed, and watch it spring back to life over the next day or two. Then, the cycle would start over. For as long as I had that plant, that was the cycle I followed—let the plant nearly die before it got my attention, then provide it some last-minute watering to keep it alive.

When we're not active in each other's lives with regularity, our building up of each other is no different than my watering routine with the plant. When I've spoken to Christians about how our churches can grow in love for one another I often receive pushback — "We already are loving." This pushback usually involves stories about how the congregation came to a fellow member's aid when they had a medical emergency, or how they all rallied around someone who was grieving a loss. All of those things are beautiful displays of love that should not be dismissed. However, if we don't go beyond that, then we're only watering the plant when it's wilting.

Two thoughts must be remembered. First, God's design wasn't just for us to be there for each other in the hour of our emergencies. He intended a constant, regular, week-in and week-out nourishment. We are to keep each other fed and strengthened. We are to pray for each other, encourage each other, and build each other up with counsel from the Word, but we can't do that if we don't know what's going on in each other's lives.

Second, though we aim to be there for each other in times of need, the truth is we're always in need. Our service, encouragement, teaching, and correction isn't a series of scheduled events but a lifestyle. As the Hebrew writer commanded us, we are to be encouraging one another day after day (Hebrews 3:13). Whether you realize it or not, you need your church family regularly bringing Christ's love and truth into your life. And, whether you (and they) realize it or not, your church family needs you to regularly bring Christ's love and truth into their lives as well.

Eventually, regularity gets seen as reliability. Most people don't just become a part of a congregation and instantly start opening themselves up to those around them. Constant encouragement and relationship-building go a long way in showing people they are loved, and people come to rely on the people who love them.

Once regularity becomes reliability, we begin fostering the culture of vulnerability. We are to confess our sins to one another and bear one another's burdens, but we don't share our burdens and sins with people unless we know we can rely on them, that we're safe with them. Consistent, Christlike love applied regularly is what it takes to earn that reliability. From there we are free to be open with each other, confessing our sins and leaning on each other. Regularity, then, is the key.

In practical terms, this looks like making a determined effort to get to spend time with others. It means being sacrificial with your time. If you don't have time to see or talk with any of your church family outside of Sunday morning, then you don't have the opportunity to obey God's commands to love one another and all the other subcommands that follow it. You won't be able to make time for your entire congregation, but you can do it for some. Pray asking for people you can love and encourage, and then work to build a rapport with them by becoming a regular in their lives. Practice regular hospitality. Grab Sunday lunch with them. Pray for and with them. Bring Christlike love into their lives. Not everybody is going to be interested, and that's just fine. Take those who are interested and show love to them. Through this you can also help disciple them, discussing the Word together, praying together, and developing a kingdom focus together.

As a church leader, this may very well mean scaling back on the church schedule. If people are constantly expected to be at the building they aren't going to have time to practice these things. It's because we have a backward, businesslike view of the church that many see attendance "every time the doors are open" as the sign of faithfulness. In the New Testament, the sign of a faithful Christian is the fruit they bear. We have to give people the training to bear fruit, and then we have to give them the time and space to do so. Yes, it's important to be at the assembly each Sunday. That should always be a non-negotiable. But the parts of the church schedule set by man should always be adaptable to the goal of glorifying Christ.

At my congregation we have some folks who rarely make Sunday night and Wednesday night gatherings at the building. Some might consider them unfaithful, wavering members. But, they are also regulars at weekly in-home fellowship times, take part in multiple personal studies each week, and are the first to volunteer every time there's a chance to serve. One of them leads multiple ministry efforts.

Some might consider this heresy, but I'm just not bothered that they aren't there on Wednesday nights. For one couple, it's one of the few nights a week they can have together. They're regularly bearing the kind of fruit God wants His people to bear. Am I supposed to say they don't care about their fellow members because they aren't there on Wednesday? They're more in tune with their fellow members than just about anybody. Am I supposed to say they aren't interested in growing? They're constantly shifting their schedule around to study with others week in and week out. In short, they're doing what Jesus did. I'm not saying that Christians should start defying church leadership and show up only when they deem necessary because they're busy with other things. I'm saying that church leadership should keep the ultimate goal in mind in creating the schedule for church life. If someone is involved in more service, fellowship, and study than the service, fellowship, and study we're trying to provide at the midweek gathering, then we're doing something right in making disciples instead of consumers.

It borders on the Pharisaical to judge people for their adherence to human traditions rather than the fruit they're bearing. How many "every time the doors are open" Christians know little about their fellow Christians? How many have perfect attendance yet don't see anybody else outside the building? Christlike love isn't about checking off the attendance box or doing something nice every now and then. It's about sacrificing our time to build each other up. Regularity is where the growth, love, and service happens. It's going to cost us our time to make it happen.

We must be sacrificial with our money and possessions.

While a kingdom-centered view of money is a topic worthy of a book all its own, I do think a few points should be highlighted here. Of greatest importance, Jesus did not care about keeping up with the Joneses. He gave up the riches of Heaven to live without a place to lay His head because that's what God's plan required. That attitude is what He expects of His followers.

I've often assured myself and crowds I've preached to that when Jesus told the rich young ruler to sell all he had, give to the poor, and come follow that such a requirement was not one given to everybody. Instead, He was just poking at the greatest idol in the ruler's heart. While that may be true, Luke 12:29-34 should not be ignored. There Jesus adds on to the phrases most often quoted from Matthew 6:20 and 6:33, "Lay up your treasures in Heaven" and "Seek first the kingdom" with an interesting twist.

"Do not fear, little flock, for it is your Father's good pleasure to give you the   kingdom. Sell what you have and give alms; provide yourselves money bags which do not grow old, a treasure in the heavens that does not fail, where no thief approaches nor moth destroys." (Luke 12:32-33)

Seeking first the kingdom and laying up our treasures in Heaven isn't just about having the right attitude about the value of possessions and God's ability to provide. It also means doing something about it, acting in such a way that it's clear we value the kingdom more than the temporal. It means cutting back on what we have when we have the chance to help others.

Again, my instinct is to start downplaying this command and take it as less than literal. But in their attempts to observe all He commanded, His disciples did exactly what Jesus described here. In Acts 2–5 we see them repeatedly selling what they had and bringing it to the Apostles to distribute to those in need. In 2 Corinthians 8 Paul commends the Macedonian Christians for having this same attitude. They were in deep poverty, yet they found a way to contribute to the needs of the saints. And, of course, we can point to Matthew 25 where Jesus insisted that those He would know in the judgment are those who are clothing, feeding, visiting, and taking in those in need.

A Jesus-centric view of our possessions leads to a church culture that is radically different than worldly culture. Where money, possessions, and experiences are some of the world's great idols, we as the church are to see those things as tools in God's hands for blessing others.

Yes, there can be abuses of this. In 2 Thessalonians 3:7-12 Paul addressed the importance of working and not being a burden on others. Having a sacrificial, kingdom view of money doesn't mean providing people the opportunity to leech off others. On the other hand, it doesn't mean taking a vow of poverty and never spending a dime. Instead, it's about our attitude toward what we have. It means having a constant eye toward blessing and caring for others out of what we've been given that goes beyond just our weekly budgeted contribution—even if we have to cut back and downsize from time to time in order to do so.

We must be sacrificial with our homes.

We live in an era where the house is totally closed off to the outside world. It is our escape, our sanctuary. All you have to do is contrast the design of houses built today and houses built 50 years ago. Not only do we not have front porches anymore, but the design has gone in the opposite direction. We live in fortresses where the living areas are being built downstairs or to the back of the house, walling us off from the world outside our front door. We then retreat inside these fortresses and connect with the outside world through social media, a terribly fake substitute for real life interaction. To love one another as Christ loved and to take the church outside of the building we're going to have to tear down those walls. (Um, metaphorically, of course.)

It's not just that "be hospitable to one another" is a command (1 Peter 4:9), but it's also one of the ways we're expected to be devoted to one another in honor (Romans 12:10-13). It's so important to God that He doesn't want men to rise to leadership positions in the church if this practice isn't part of their lives (1 Timothy 3:2, Titus 1:8). Why is it so important?

When it comes to helping people grow in Christ, the kitchen table can be just as effective as the pulpit—possibly even more. It's in the informal setting of the home that we can share questions, help people learn at their own level and pace, and pray specific prayers together. It's where

Jesus did much of His teaching. It's where discipleship has a chance to take off. And, it's a fantastic tool for evangelism. It gives us the opportunity to introduce people to the church as Jesus' people rather than as an organization for them to either like or dislike.

One of my very favorite things about growing up in my parents' house was their dedication to hospitality. We had fairly regular get togethers where literally dozens of Christians were in our home for a meal. At other times we would have another Christian family or two over for dinner and sit around the table late into the night discussing the Bible, the church, the culture, and all kinds of other topics. I remember young mothers giving my mom a call and asking if they could come over and pick her brain about parenting, education, or anything else they needed help with. It was (and still is) a fairly regular occurrence for Christian friends to come in from out of town and call to ask if they could stay, leading to more time of fellowship and deep conversation.

Just posting a picture of their house on social media when I go back for a visit has led to all kinds of Christian friends commenting to reminisce about times of fellowship there. I know it's been a blessing to the dozens (if not hundreds) who have come through. I know it's been a blessing to my parents, and it's been a blessing to me. I learned early and often the importance of Christian fellowship. I grew from the conversations in which I got to listen and later participate. It's that sense of family and the realization that some of the deepest growth comes from long, Bible-focused conversation that showed me church could be more. It's the disparity between the feeling of coming home from a Sunday morning with little sense of community versus a night of table fellowship that shows why it's so important to spend that extra time together.

However, a few concerns arise whenever this topic is discussed. "My house is never clean enough to have people over," some have said. It doesn't matter if your house is sparkling clean or if you're having one of those weeks where the laundry and dishes just won't ever end. Letting people in our imperfect houses is actually a great metaphor for how church life should work. We're letting each other see that our lives aren't

Instagram perfect. By doing this we're showing that our fellowship isn't defined by preserving a perfect facade. We're saying instead that loving each other and building each other up are more important than making everyone think our lives are flawless.

If you want to host others for meals, cost can also become an issue. Rest assured, it doesn't have to be anything fancy. It doesn't matter if you can provide prime rib or peanut butter and jellies. What matters is that the family has a chance to be with each other and build the kind of relationships where the one anothers can be fulfilled. But even feeding people inexpensive meals with any regularity can be a strain if the budget is tight. So get creative with it. Cut out a trip to a restaurant once a month with the faith that God will bless what we give up for Him and His work. Plenty of folks don't even have that kind of expense to cut, though. An option in that case: plan a shared meal where each person or family brings their own. Once again, the message is being sent that what matters is being together and not showing off. Another option might be to take $5 or so off your weekly contribution and put it toward having some brothers and sisters over for a meal and a time of devotional and prayer once a month. Some church leaders probably aren't terribly happy with that suggestion, but it gets at the heart of thinking of the church as a family rather than an organization. Doing such isn't "taking away from the work of the church." It's doing the work of the church as an active participant.

If you want to feel truly blessed and truly bless others, make time for hospitality and table fellowship. To grow and to help others grow, work on developing relationships that go beyond the building. Use the resources God has given you to model Jesus, teach Jesus, and show others how to do the work of Jesus.

We must be sacrificial with our comfort.

First, we have to give up our carefully cultivated image. Discipleship, growth, and the one anothers don't happen without us opening ourselves up and letting others truly know us. This isn't a flaw in the design;

it's a foundational piece of God's plan. Such openness keeps us humble, reliant on His grace, and leaning on each other.

It's been said that one of the great flaws of the social media era is that we compare our behind-the-scenes with everyone else's highlight reel. We put the best of ourselves out on social media while in real life the struggles are still all too real. What we need is to be loved for who we really are and not for our highlight reel. God doesn't just love the cleaned-up version of ourselves we present to the world. His love wouldn't be very valuable if that's all it covered. Instead, He knows everything about us and still loves us just the same. That's what we are to offer one another.

As long as we only connect in passing, we can preserve the safe, carefully cultivated image we want others to see. We can answer "How are you?" with "Good!" each Sunday morning, no matter how deep our struggles may be that week. If we're going to practice confessing our sins to one another, bearing one another's burdens, and letting others bear our burdens, by necessity we'll have to commit to going beyond that to let ourselves be truly known. When you open your life up and invite others in, they're going to see the moments of marital conflict, the struggles with sin, the days where we're short on patience. That picture of the lovely, well-put-together home we've given everyone is going to be shattered from time to time. This is the trade we've been called to make if we want the treasure of the kingdom.

As a deeply introverted person, this is a great struggle. I'm perfectly fine just sitting back and keeping to myself. On top of that, as a preacher the struggle is even greater. As a minister it can feel dangerous to open up about our flaws. Unfortunately, it's not unheard of for ministers to lose their jobs after admitting to sins. At the very least it will change the way people think of us. So, there are certainly considerations to the way we handle these things. I don't think it would be wise to make each Christian get up in front of a room full of people and tell everyone their deepest, darkest struggles. However, if we're dedicated to growing closer to one another, we won't be able to hold on to our perfect facades for long. Thus, the decision has to be made: sacrifice the image I've cultivated for the sake of promoting Christ, or hang on to my comfort. Jesus taught us that if we're striving for the praise of men we'd better be happy with it because that's the only reward we're getting. In order to model Christ for others, we have to empty ourselves. As with all of these things, the message is that though it hurts, it's eternally worth it.

Second, we have to learn to give consideration. It's our default state to see the world through our own eyes. It takes practice to see others' point of view. The disciple should be taught both by word and by example just how important it is to consider how what we say and do affects those around us. Each Christian must grow into the habit of considering what will "give grace to those who hear" (Ephesians 4:29) around our Christian family and seasoning our speech with the salt of grace (Colossians 4:6) among the lost. Will I be a stumbling block? What does the weaker brother need from me? Does this edify or tear down? What kind of example am I setting? The Christ-following Christian knows he is not living for himself.

One practical application of this comes in the form of consideration on social media. Every day I scroll by posts from Christians that mock their political opponents as stupid or evil. Even worse, many of those posts tell the poster's opponents to unfriend them. How is this behavior Christlike? It may be our preference to broadcast our opinions. It may be our tendency to think less of those who disagree. But following Jesus means thinking beyond our petty preferences and opinions to more eternal concerns. What is good for the souls of those around me? Will this hurt my relationship with a brother or sister? Will this drive the lost away from Christ? As Paul taught in the discussions regarding the eating of meats sacrificed to idols, just because we have the right to do something doesn't mean we should. "All things are lawful for me, but not all things are helpful; all things are lawful for me, but not all things edify. Let no one seek his own, but each one the other's well-being" (1 Corinthians 10:23-24). This attitude that focuses on what is truly important above our own preferences is critical to the unity of the church. The disciple needs to be taught such consideration and have it modeled by those who lead them.

Third, we have to learn to listen. Our natural inclination might be to express our opinion, share a story we have, or turn the conversation back to our preferences and understandings. Bearing one another's burdens, encouraging each other day after day, and turning each other from sin requires dedication to this skill that is hard to come by these days. Loving others means deferring to others in conversation and showing them we care about them by hearing them out.

Fourth — and this is a tough one — the Christ follower must learn to be loving in confrontation. In order to stir one another up to love and good works (Hebrews 10:24), sometimes we're going to have to show each other a better way. On the other side of that coin, we must learn to accept correction. It's not easy to be told we're in the wrong or need to change in some way, but it's an essential part of our growth and close relationships. We all have blind spots and need others to help us see them. The point of these two thoughts is not to create a culture of criticism and tearing each other down. The key to this loving, peaceful correction is a shared agreement that the goal is to help each other be like Christ. This primes us for growth in ways that just aren't possible when our goal is to defend ourselves and preserve a flawless image of ourselves. The only cost is our comfort.

THE GREATEST TRADE YOU'LL EVER MAKE

The ultimate end of all these things is to be a community of people who are living out Christ's example. There are some thoughts here that might be uncomfortable. Quite frankly, some of them make me uncomfortable. If it's a Biblically driven discomfort, though, that's a good thing. Without discomfort we would never be able to break out of the rut of consumeristic Christianity. Everything about Jesus' life was counter to our instinct to put self first. Following Him means going against the grain and doing things that don't make a whole lot of sense to our human minds.

The key idea that links all of these together and that the New Testament establishes consistently is this: Whatever we trade for the kingdom will be more than worth it, both here and throughout eternity. As Jesus reassured Peter when Peter reminded the Lord of the disciples' sacrifices,

> Assuredly, I say to you, there is no one who has left house or brothers or sisters or father or mother or wife or children or lands, for My sake and the gospel's, who shall not receive a hundredfold now in this time—houses and brothers and sisters and mothers and children and lands, with persecutions—and in the age to come, eternal life. But many who are first will be last, and the last first.
>
> Mark 10:29-31

If you think about the beauty of not just living in God's presence but being surrounded by our brothers and sisters as we have all been cleansed of all selfishness and love each other for all eternity, it's a powerful thought. As you study the kingdom, though, it becomes clear that God intended those benefits to begin now. No, it won't be as perfect as it will be one day, but we can begin to have a taste of it here (often described as the "already but not yet" dichotomy of the kingdom). Everybody wants to go to Heaven, but it's important we realize God has provided us a chance to get a head start on it in this life. That can only happen when we deny ourselves and teach others to do the same.

DISCUSSION QUESTIONS

1. How do you think the sacrifices required of Christians today compare with the sacrifices made by Christians in the New Testament church?

2. Which of the sacrifices discussed in this chapter is the biggest challenge for you?

3. What is a practical way you can show sacrificial love to someone in your life?

12

QUESTIONS

Christianity is not for loners or individualists. It is for a people traveling together down the narrow path that leads to life. You must follow and you must lead. You must be loved and you must love. And we love others best by helping them to follow Jesus down the pathway of life.

Mark Dever[1]

IT'S IMPORTANT THAT A realistic view be established before concluding. While many of us have dreamed of something more for the church and many are excited to be on that journey, that doesn't mean we're promised a smooth path where everything goes perfectly. Still, there is reason to be excited despite the challenges we face. In this chapter we'll examine some questions that have been raised and some of the concerns I've found in my own experience, but also the reasons for opti-

1. Mark Dever, *Discipling: How to Help Others Follow Jesus,* Wheaton: Crossway, 2016, Kindle Edition. 13.

mism that a shift in church practice can bring.

QUESTIONS

What if my congregation doesn't want to?

Some of the folks I've spoken with in the writing process have expressed frustration that their congregation doesn't seem interested in building relationships or studying the Bible outside of the building. I'm sure there are others who will read this book and want to see changes come to pass, only to find that others are hesitant to make such changes. I can relate to both of those feelings. It can be frustrating to feel as though something that's so important to us doesn't matter to those who we feel should be helping us.

While every situation is different, a few points should be considered. The most important thing I can say is that we must never be divisive in our efforts to serve Christ. Pulling away from a church family because they don't meet our standards or undermining an eldership because they don't see eye to eye with us is one of the least Christlike things we can do. On the other hand, just because your leadership has other plans does not mean you can't obey God's commands as you understand them. First, if you can be hospitable, do so. The time spent with fellow Christians is never a waste, even if they don't reciprocate or see it as important. Second, go out of your way to stay in contact with your church family. While there are those who might not respond to the attention, there will always be those who appreciate the concern shown to them. That can be a launching place for deeper relationships. Third, seek to either be discipled or to make a disciple. Pray for God to put someone in your life to disciple you or whom you can disciple. If you're seeking to do God's will out of a pure heart, trust that He will bless you with opportunity to do so. He might put a fellow Christian in your path, or it might be someone who is yet to come to Christ. Keep the Great Commission cycle in mind, with the goal being to turn one or two disciple-makers into many. Even though God's work can be frustrating and lonely, He grows us through those times. He builds our patience and faith, and He rewards our efforts to serve Him.

What about the failures of past discipleship efforts?

Unfortunately, with the mention of disciple-making some will instantly have a negative reaction. In the last 50 years the International Church of Christ (also known as the Boston Movement and the Crossroads Movement) rose up with a heavy emphasis on discipleship and disciple-making that led to fairly rapid growth. With that growth, though, came extreme discipling practices that bordered on cult-like. They, too, emphasized relationships, evangelizing, and following Christ, but their abuses provide a cautionary tale of how easily these practices can become dangerously misapplied. Look them up online and you'll find horrifying stories of people who had their lives controlled by mentors and "prayer partners" in the name of discipleship. Many had friends and family members cut off by the church and were constantly guilted into confessing sins, whether real or imagined. It's understandable that some would be incredibly nervous about an emphasis on disciple-making.

We certainly should take precautions to avoid such practices, and the best way to do so is to look at others' mistakes and learn from them. There are two key areas to watch. First, we must maintain the Bible's emphasis on humble, servant leadership. Anywhere an authority structure becomes too top-heavy, abuse is inevitable. It's not an "if" but a "when." That's when people start making decisions for others and start dominating their lives to make them fit a vision the leadership demands. Some will take advantage of those under them for personal gain. Instead, Jesus-like servant leadership must be the church's emphasis.

Second, we must pay attention to whether we're cultivating a community of grace or fear. Fear is man's way of manipulating people to act as we think they should. Grace is God's way of giving us the patience we need to keep going when we fall. The stories that come out of such groups often include fear as a driving force for subjugation, holding hell, relationships, reputation, or anything else that matters to people over their heads. We are to withdraw from the unrepentant in our midst, not try to ruin their lives. There certainly is reason to fear if we stray from God's Word, but the point of the community is to lovingly rebuke us, not control us.

However, an incorrect practice of disciple-making—no matter how dangerously incorrect it may be—must not drive us away from applying the Great Commission. Disciple-making is a non-negotiable part of God's plan for the church.

What about the danger of burnout?

In the previous chapter we looked at the Christian's call to be self-sacrificial with our time. However, that doesn't mean every free hour of our schedules needs to be booked for hospitality, service, or studies. If you're married and/or have kids, it should be non-negotiable to have time for your family in the schedule. Plenty of ministers have driven away their families by spending all their time focusing on others at the expense of their family. It would be foolish for any Christian to repeat their mistakes, let alone every Christian.

The point in being sacrificial with our time is to do so out of love for others, but love for others must also include our families. Jesus got away from the crowds every now and then. It's important that we do that for ourselves and our families, too. So, while we shouldn't dodge commitment to the church by over-committing ourselves to our hobbies and our kids and their activities, we also shouldn't get so tied up in God's work that we forget that our families are part of God's work for us, too. It's up to each home to find a balance between spending quality time with each other and making time for the church family and for serving God.

What if I live far away?

Most cities (particularly in the Bible belt) offer a number of options when it comes time to choose a congregation of believers. Because of this, it's fairly common for people to drive 30 minutes to an hour each Sunday, often passing multiple congregations on their way. Because all of these options are available, and because we choose the one that's the best fit for us, it's easy to end up in a situation where all of our church friends will generally be our same race, social status, and age, and with almost the exact same beliefs about everything, which seems foreign to everything the church was intended to be (see Galatians 3:28, for one).

The solution? When you have to choose, unless there is a clear Biblical reason against doing so, join the church that is nearest to your house. Why?

First, the further you travel to worship, the more difficult fellowship and service become. It's hard enough to find time to get together with our Christian family outside of Sundays and Wednesdays, and events at the building can be difficult to squeeze into our schedule. Add an hour round trip to the equation and it becomes incredibly easy to be minimally involved in the lives of your fellow Christians. When someone needs a visit or a meal, that's a steep time commitment and you might not be able to help out very often. If you're trying to be more hospitable, it might be difficult for them to drive all the way to your home. I'm not saying it can't be done or that it isn't done, but it certainly adds a degree of difficulty which can be limiting. On the other hand, if we go into the decision of where to worship by asking "Where can I best serve?" rather than "Which church is most aligned with what I want and need?" it makes a strong case for staying local.

Second, it can add to the difficulty of evangelism. It's much harder to convince someone to go to worship or an informal study with you (and especially to consider doing so regularly) if it's all the way across town. It's equally difficult to try to introduce them to the church family. Beyond that, it's another question to have to answer. People often want to know why our church is different from those all around, and in this scenario we then have to explain why we chose not just our particular type of church but why that particular congregation over others of the same beliefs.

Third, and possibly most importantly, determining to fit in with the nearest congregation is crucial to overcoming the consumer Christianity mindset. Once major doctrinal questions are out of the way, people typically choose where to attend based on what churches have to offer. Basically, churches are asked "What can you do to earn my membership?" Instead, we should be looking for the best place to serve and function as part of the body. And, it's my contention that that place will typically be the nearest congregation. That's partly because of the reasons named above–fellowship, serving, and evangelism. But it's also because it causes us to go into the situation with a determination to get along. When we go in with a view to find a church that is the custom fit for who we are and what we desire, we minimize the Bible's commands to bear with one another, tolerate one another in love, and accept each other despite differences of opinion.

Please realize that I'm not calling for any major doctrinal compromises. In any case beyond that, though, it's important to keep in mind that despite our individual differences we're on the same team when it comes to the Gospel. If there's anything to be learned from Philippians it's that there is great joy to be had when we work through difficult situations and personal differences for the sake of the church and its purposes. But that doesn't happen when we seek out situations that cater to us, or when we determine to adjust as little as possible. When we drive past congregations to find one that suits us better, the implied message is, "You're my brethren, and we're going to spend eternity together, but because we have slightly different preferences let's just keep to our separate circles here on earth."

On the other hand, when we reject this mindset it gives us the constant reminder that church isn't about us. The message of Romans 14 was not "go find the congregation that has your views on holidays, meats, or drinking," but "accept each other, don't judge each other on matters of opinion, and build each other up." Being part of a family isn't always easy, and it almost always brings challenges to our preferences, but we're better for it in the end. If you're thinking that you'd like to be more involved with your church family but are too far away, it might be time to think over your options.

What about the events we have?

I'll admit I've been pretty hard on lectureships, Gospel meetings, workshops, and other such events in this book. That doesn't mean they're inherently wrong. I'm not here to dictate your church schedule. The point is simply this: we must know our goal, and we must act consistently in pursuit of it. If we have the goal of bringing as many people as possible to maturity in Christ, then we should act consistently with that goal. We should plan in such a way to achieve that goal, and we should evaluate whether the things we do are supporting that goal or detracting from it. A special event may very well help achieve that goal.

In the best cases the event serves as a launching point for further activity, study, and growth. The trouble is in letting those things become a substitute, when the meeting is held *instead of* relationship-based discipleship. A seminar on a topic like finance, marriage, apologetics, or parenting, for example, can be a beneficial thing, but it also can't possibly solve everyone's problems or bring people to maturity in a weekend. With our goal in mind, we must use such things as a springboard to greater growth rather than as a quick fix.

WARNINGS

In addition to the questions that may arise, I'd like to offer a few warnings from my own experience with regard to a change in practice.

Avoid the appeal of cliques.

One of the biggest challenges to positive momentum is the formation of cliques. A few spiritually-minded people connect with each other and find kinship in a shared passion for Biblical things. They grow in fellowship and service to one another—not unlike that which was described in an earlier chapter. However, it fails to extend beyond the group. Others are excluded either by lack of invitation or by inability to fit in with the group. The group can even develop a holier-than-thou view toward other members who apparently must not be as interested in God as those in the clique, as the thinking goes. Sadly, I've fallen into such behavior before. I can tell you from experience that it's not healthy for those in the group and will do nothing to bless those outside the group.

Such exclusionary practices are antithetical to Christlikeness. If all the self-appointed spiritually mature are keeping themselves separate from the immature, it's a sure sign those in the first group aren't all that mature to begin with. Cliques don't look to bring people to Christ, they seek to protect their own comfort. On the other hand, with making disciples as the goal, we should constantly be looking to bring in more people, connect them to the family, and teach them to be like Christ. Those who come to maturity will realize they've been called to bless and train others rather than constantly be fed by other mature people. Therefore, the group should be constantly growing and changing. That means we won't get to spend all our time exclusively with the same group of friends for years and years. And, it means we won't always get to hand-pick our group of friends based on our personal interests and preferences. But, we trust the promise that when we pursue God's plan we'll be far more blessed than when we pursue our own.

Don't expect overnight change.

Like most good things we attempt in life—losing weight, earning a living, learning new skills—there isn't a shortcut, and if there were a shortcut it almost certainly wouldn't bring lasting improvement. Jesus had the shortcut option at His disposal numerous times when big crowds followed Him, but He never took it. He stayed committed to His path of training a few who could go train others. There is no quick path to bringing a person to maturity in Christ, which means there's also no quick path to bringing an entire congregation to maturity in Christ. I've certainly tried, making efforts like preaching entire series on the Great Commission to help Christians see the importance of it. As you might imagine, "Guys, we have to get out there and make disciples" had little effect. I might as well have said "Guys, we have to get out there and build an oak spiral staircase." If they haven't been taught previously, then it's just not going to happen. They may very well be able to build one eventually, but there's nothing I can say in 30 minutes that's going to make it possible. (To be fair, I have no idea how to build an oak spiral staircase, either.)

As it's been said many times in many places, disciples are hand-made. That's how Jesus did it, that's how Paul did it, that's how Elijah did it, and that's how we have to do it. Because disciples are hand-made, a church culture of loving, family-like Jesus-followers can not be built any faster than the disciples are made. Like the mustard seed of Jesus' parable (Matthew 13:31-32), that which starts small can yield great results. We just have to stick with it and avoid the allure of the shortcut.

Don't expect perfection.

It's important to temper our excitement with the reminder that there is no path to a church culture where everything goes exactly as we want it to and nothing bad ever happens. Humans are involved, and we're imperfect, so there are going to be problems. One of the most important things to keep in mind is that we should not expect perfection. Up to this point the entirety of this book has been spent discussing how much more church could be if we follow God's design. However, if we're not careful with our dreaming and our efforts we can turn the church into an idol. If the goal is to find the perfect situation, all we will do is get frustrated and migrate from one place to another or berate those around us until we realize our goal. That's why the perfect situation can't be our goal. Rather, the goal is to be like Jesus and to help others do the same, and being like Jesus includes a lot of grace, humility, and love. He was patient with us. We must be patient with others.

Dietrich Bonhoeffer said it best in *Life Together*, his book on the beauty of Christian community.

> The serious Christian, set down for the first time in a Christian community, is likely to bring with him a very definite idea of what Christian life together should be and to try to realize it. But God's grace speedily shatters such dreams. Just as God desires to lead us to a knowledge of

genuine Christian fellowship, so surely must we be overwhelmed by a great disillusionment with others, with Christians in general, and, if we are fortunate, with ourselves… The sooner this shock of disillusionment comes to an individual and to a community the better for both. A community which cannot bear and cannot survive such a crisis, which insists upon keeping its illusion when it should be shattered, permanently loses in that moment the promise of Christian community. Sooner or later it will collapse. Every human wish dream that is injected into the Christian community is a hindrance to genuine community and must be banished if genuine community is to survive. He who loves his dream of community itself becomes a destroyer of the latter, even though his personal intentions may be ever so honest and earnest and sacrificial.[2]

The warning against a "wish dream" church has to remain ever present in our minds. The thought of creating such a wish dream for you, the reader, was one of my biggest hesitations in writing and publishing this book. The last thing I want is someone criticizing their elders and looking down on their brethren because the church isn't acting in the way that this book has attempted to outline as the Biblical view.

On the other hand, if it leads to the disillusionment Bonhoeffer mentioned, good can come of it. It's in those disillusioning moments that our heart is revealed. If things move more slowly than I'd like, if people don't act the way I think they should, if there isn't perfect harmony, what will I do? My goal cannot be to make people act as I deem they must. My goal must be to emulate Christ and help others do the same and then let God handle the rest. If I only love them when they're perfectly in line with me, I don't love them with the love of Christ. The disillusionment helps us see that neither we nor the people around us are perfect imitators of Christ, which should humble us and make us realize the importance of

---

2. Dietrich Bonhoeffer, *Life Together: The Classic Exploration of Christian Community*, New York: Harper & Row Publishers, Inc., 1954. 27.

grace and patience.

A hope for something better

On the other hand, the realization that perfection won't be reached here in this life doesn't mean we can't hope for and work toward a more Biblical version of church. There are plenty of reasons to be excited about what could be as we let God's Word lead. I believe many of the biggest issues facing the church in recent years are greatly mitigated by following God's plan. A few examples:

Youth unfaithfulness

I would argue the biggest issue facing the church today is the youth dropout rate. We are losing young people by the thousands and have been for years. This issue often gets downplayed or disputed by those who live in cities near bigger congregations and don't see a problem. Nearly every church they see has a youth group and the camps and conferences always have plenty of young people. However, there are plenty of smaller, more rural churches with essentially no youth presence whatsoever. Outside of those concentrated areas you will find plenty of congregations without anybody under 20 years old. Sometimes there will be young children, but they're being toted to worship by their grandparents as the parents and the rest of the 20-40 year olds are nowhere to be found. That's not only what the eye test tells us but what the researchers have also long confirmed. The studies have varied greatly in their findings, but nearly all of them have reported that over half of those who grow up in a Christian home will walk away from the faith.

The reasons given always vary, but some of the more common ones are that the young people never developed a faith of their own, they were never taught to defend what they believe, and they never developed intergenerational relationships. In a system where young people are baptized and stashed away for years in a junior varsity version of church where they are largely separate from the rest of their Christian family, it's no wonder that each of these leading factors are in play. For me, despite growing up as a regular attendee of a faithful congregation, after baptism there was little expected of me outside of showing up to classes and events or going to camps. Occasionally I was asked to say a prayer during Sunday night worship or pass out communion trays on Sunday morning. Outside of our respective parents, nobody was really discipling me or my peers individually. There was simply a one-size-fits-all program to attend until graduation.

On the other hand, a system in which young people find mentorship and a Jesus-focused plan for their spiritual growth is an answer to these shortcomings. With people who will teach them to study, teach them to pray, answer their questions, and make them part of the family, they have a far better chance of survival than when they are told to come to classes and devos in hopes that the message will stick. Intergenerational relationships, Biblical convictions, and opportunities for service give young people the deep roots they need to stay faithful as they grow into adulthood.

Women's roles

One of the most prominent issues of the 21st century has been and will continue to be the role of women in the church. Many are pushing for full participation in leadership and worship. Others, of course, disagree, while still others are advocating some kind of compromise. While this book is not meant to provide an in-depth discussion of that issue, there is reason to believe a more Biblical church would alleviate some of the challenges levied against male-led churches.

When "church" is 90% or so focused on what happens in the building on Sunday, and women aren't allowed to participate there, then it's not unfair to say that women are second class citizens of sorts. If, on the other hand, the Sunday gathering is just one part (an important part, but still one of many) of what the church does, we can meaningfully say, "Women are allowed to do nearly everything but that."

Spiritually-minded, older Christian women are commanded to share their wisdom with younger Christian women (Titus 2:4), and the younger women would be wise to seek them out. No, it's not a sermon, but the impact of discipling a woman and thereby impacting her husband, children, grandchildren and everyone with whom she comes into contact can be far greater. They might not occupy the pulpit, but their teaching is still desperately needed. The Bible shows the power of praying, worshiping women with the examples of Miriam, Hannah, and Anna, along with Mary's "Magnificat." They might not be authorized to lead worship, but their worship and prayer matters.

The women who followed and ministered to Jesus throughout the Gospels played a vital role in His ministry despite the fact that they weren't chosen in the Twelve. God's work can be wonderfully administered by faithful women in a number of ways that don't have to include the Sunday gathering. You probably have a Christian woman from your life coming to mind who has joyfully embraced this role and impacted a congregation by her faithfulness. Though such women might not have a title, they are certainly needed servants of the church.

In the age of Google searches and Facebook groups, it's easy for all of us to look to internet strangers for advice and spiritual encouragement, and young women are no exception. But what they need more than anything is to have women in their own congregations who care for them and are intentional about being in their lives. Women might not be able to be elders, but they can still guide and care for souls. Therefore, it's vitally important that we create a culture that goes beyond Sundays and beyond the building.

Christianity's outward image

It's no stretch to say that Christianity is growing increasingly unpopular in our culture, but there are two sides to that coin. In one sense, that's not a strike against us; in fact, it's quite the opposite. The world is always going to have a problem with Jesus and His people (John 15:18-19). The Gospel is offensive because it tells people their self-applied standard of righteousness is invalid. Anybody who upholds this truth by insisting that Jesus is Lord will not receive the culture's approval.

In another sense, though, we haven't helped ourselves. Because the

Gospel is offensive enough on its own we have to be extremely cautious not to add offense to it. Unfortunately, for multiple generations Christianity has become commonly seen as a political movement or a holier-than-thou group of people in an ivory tower church building. We say that church is the people rather than the building, but to most unchurched outsiders they identify different churches by location. To those who have a degree of Biblical literacy, they identify different churches by each one's defining doctrinal characteristics, such as how a church worships. Sadly, they often don't know us as their neighbors who love them and who are an image of Christlikeness in their lives. We can't change everyone's minds all at once, but by getting outside of our buildings and working on showing people the love of Christ by building relationships with them we can help change their perception of us.

Minister burnout

Minister burnout is a very real, very dangerous side effect of a church model in which the preacher bears the responsibility for the success or failure of a business. With customers (members) always tugging at him to get their way, and with managers (elders) determining whether his approval rating is high enough to keep him around, it's no wonder so many ministers struggle with depression and anxiety. When so many view their minister as an employee of an organization they attend, it's no wonder he and his family are often so lonely.

This is yet another problem that is improved when the preacher gets to be just one part of a functioning church body rather than the key piece who is tasked with driving the lion's share of the church's work. Rather than trying to appease countless people who remain in spiritual infancy and require constant attention, the minister should have people who can share in the work and who can in turn care for him as well. Every preacher knows the value of the Christians who show love and consideration for the minister and his family. In the Biblical system where people are being brought to maturity, those encouraging, life-giving people aren't quite as few and far between.

Mental health

One of the most widely discussed issues of our day is the crisis of mental health struggles. People all around us struggle with depression, anxiety, and other challenges. In many (if not most) cases, if the person next to us in the pew on Sunday is fighting such a battle, we'll never know about it. God's design for the church gives us an opportunity to be on the front lines of helping each other through such troubles, though.

This is not to downplay the importance of therapy and medicines where needed, but a church family that loves like Jesus and remains a constant in each other's lives is one of the best tools a person can have in their fight for good mental health. We all need to be loved despite our shortcomings, and a church family with which we can be open and share our struggles gives us that. We all need an identity, and an identity grounded in the cross is the best identity a person can have. We all need purpose to keep us going, and a church family that depends on "what every joint supplies" gives us that. The person in the midst of the struggles gets the chance to contribute to others rather than feeling like they are somebody's pet project. Such love, belonging, and purpose can go a long way toward helping each other. It's yet another reason why God's design was so brilliant for fighting the battles presented by a fallen world full of sickness and pain.

Overlooked groups

It's heartbreaking how many people have a story of struggling to fit in with a church family. Sometimes the demographics line up in such a way to leave people feeling like they don't belong. Singles, those who are divorced, and those who are childless are just a few who sometimes struggle to fit in. There is certainly value in groups that are created for those in such categories as their shared experiences can create a sense of understanding and belonging they might not find elsewhere. However, separating them from the rest of the group is certainly not the picture the New Testament paints. We are all one in Christ. We share each other's burdens, weeping with those weep and making them part of the family. Jesus always noticed the downtrodden that the common society had passed over. Jesus-following disciples do the same and refuse to let them stay overlooked or excluded.

Pornography addiction

Pornography addiction has beset countless spiritual lives, and the problem isn't going to just go away on its own in a time when kids are practically born with a WiFi-enabled device in their hands. It's a sin that thrives on shame and secrecy, and we were ill-equipped to handle its transition to the internet. "If you need to confess a sin, come forward as we stand and sing" does no good to people who are fighting a sin that carries such a strong stigma.

By being the church as God designed it, though, we have exactly what we need to defeat this epidemic. Pornography is defeated by strong relationships that offer both love and accountability. Only when we establish the kind of love and trust God wants us to offer each other will there be a climate where people are comfortable confessing their hidden struggles. They need to know those struggles won't be held against them and that they will still be loved even when they fall. The same holds true for any number of other taboo sins.

IT'S NOT POSSIBLE TO foresee every challenge that will come our way, but it's important to be realistic in our hopes for the church. If we idolize our picture of the church, we're setting ourselves up for disappointment and we will likely negatively impact the church. Still, even among the realism there is great cause for excitement. Jesus planned His church beautifully, and the more closely we follow Him the more blessings we will see. What else can we do but praise Him?

DISCUSSION QUESTIONS

1. What are other questions you have about a shift in church tactics?

2. What other concerns should be monitored?

3. What is a problem you feel is facing the church? How do you think a relationship-based, mission-minded church structure might help the problem?

CONCLUSION

"WE DON'T GO TO church, we *are* the church."

The phrase has been around for as long as I can remember, but it's rarely been more than just a vague saying that sounds nice but lacks any teeth. We can all agree the statement is true, but that still leaves us to decide what it means in practical terms. That's why it's so exciting to see a growing movement aimed at defining what it means to be the church and then acting on that definition. It's my prayer that this book is another step in that direction for each reader.

Change is hard to come by, though. Many struggle with great discomfort at the very thought of change, resisting it at every turn. At some point most Christians have likely heard the phrase "We've always done it that way" used as a reason to not rethink methods of the past. Many are also protective of their traditions, because the longer a tradition has been in place, the easier it is to think of as a Scriptural necessity. But God does not have to be hindered by our stubbornness. Sometimes when we're shaken out of our comfort zones He takes the opportunity to do some of His best work. I do not presume to speak for God, but that may very well be what He's doing in real time as I write this conclusion.

I began writing *Church Reset* around September 2019. When I began, plenty of rethinking and changing were taking place, but nobody could have predicted what was going to happen in our world in the months to come. As words and phrases like "coronavirus," COVID-19," "social distancing," and "an abundance of caution" entered our vocabulary, church life got turned on its head. Though I have no way of knowing what the future holds on the other side of the quarantine, I have hope that God will bring wonderful changes to His church through this time. The situation has already been a catalyst for readjusting our focus on what is really important. As we've lost access to our buildings we've realized that church never was the building. As we've watched worship services online we've figured out just how hollow that experience can be without each other's presence. As our church events have been canceled and plans have been changed we've had a chance to see that the real work of the church is found in the way we connect with each other and those around us. All of this represents an opportunity to begin applying the principles we know to be true.

What forms that will take, I don't know, but I can't wait to see the ideas brought forth by those striving to restore God's plan for the church. Plenty of examples already existed before the pandemic, and more will surely come as we sort out that which must be included from that which does not serve the purpose of pointing people to Jesus and bringing us closer together. For some congregations it has meant rearranging the auditorium to have everyone facing each other, like a family does. For others it has meant giving up the building entirely. For some it has meant rearranging their Sunday schedule to allow for more fellowship and to truly treat it like a family reunion. For others it has meant rethinking the method of distributing the Lord's Supper to highlight its importance as a true *communion* meal of remembrance to be shared together rather than as individuals. For some it has meant removing lines of separation in church gatherings that have kept different ages and demographics apart.

For others it has meant rethinking the budget to cut down on overhead as much as possible in order to maximize their ability to reach the lost and help the poor. Most important of all, many have joined in the journey of making disciples, whether by gathering a group of a few or by taking on one disciple at a time. There are all kinds of things we can do to change and grow in our methods while staying within Scriptural bounds. What matters is that we stay true to the purposes for which we exist as the church in the first place.

As I've said repeatedly, this book has not been written as a step-by-step guide. I'm not looking to hold myself up as any kind of example, because I'm just another person on the same journey. All I set out to do in this book was to study the principles the Bible gives us for the church and see how those principles answer our problem of rampant consumerism in the modern American church. The different applications are up to you. It was obvious from the outset of my study that we needed to get away from building-oriented, schedule-oriented Christianity. It was also obvious that the "choose-your-own-adventure" Christianity of our individualist society was not what God ever intended. The question that remained was, how will things change? How can we drop those obviously incorrect versions of Christianity in favor of a mission-minded, family-oriented version of church?

The answer, of course, is Jesus. Every December we hear from those clamoring to "Keep Christ in Christmas." Maybe it's time we start campaigning instead to keep Christ in Christianity. Where we have drifted from our purpose it has been because we have attempted to put something other than Jesus at the center of it all. The only path back is to once again acknowledge Him as the King of everything and center everything we do on Him. What makes Christianity different from every other religion is that it has Jesus and the others do not. Christianity's Head was and is sinless. He has power over sickness, demons, nature, and even death. He is God. That's the principle I hope has been the foundational takeaway for each reader—we have to base everything we do on the beauty and supremacy of Christ. His love, His blood, His headship, His promises, and everything else about Him are where we find the power of Christianity. May we as His church look to Him, drop everything that hinders us, and run toward Him with all our might (Hebrews 12:1-2), and bring as many along with us on the journey as we can. Only then will we see just how much more church can be.

Made in the USA
Monee, IL
14 March 2024

55082823R00104